1979

THE DARKEST YEAR

A Time for Greatness
The Unquiet Years: U.S.A. 1945–1955
The Saving Remnant
The Perils of Democracy
The United States:
The Presidents, the Parties and the Constitution
The People's Choice
Abraham Lincoln
Declaration of Faith
Pursuit of Happiness:
The Story of American Democracy
Milton and Plato

THE DARKEST YEAR

Britain Alone
June 1940 - June 1941

———◆———

HERBERT AGAR

DOUBLEDAY & COMPANY, INC.
GARDEN CITY, NEW YORK   1973

Photographs 1–10, 12, 14–23 courtesy of
United Press International
Photograph 11 courtesy of Studio Schall
Photograph 13 courtesy of Imperial War Museum

ISBN: 0-385-04500-x

Library of Congress Catalog Card Number 72–96224
Copyright © 1972 by Herbert Agar
Printed in the United States of America
All Rights Reserved
First Edition in the United States of America

For Barbie

Contents

THE DARKEST YEAR

Preface

1

This is a personal book, inspired by an American's affection for England which began in 1922.

My theme is simple. From June 22, 1940, when the Germans accepted the French petition for an armistice, until June 22, 1941, when Hitler invaded Russia, there was only Britain to save the West. That period of still hardly credible survival is what I have called the lonely year.

The British could not have won the war alone, but there would have been no war to win had Britain joined France in surrender in 1940. It would have been all over. Hitler could then have dealt with Russia in his own time and the United States could not even have landed in Europe, or bombed Europe, or hindered the Nazis in any way, without Britain as a place from which to start.

My first-hand contribution is what happened in the United States, among war-mongers, during 1940 and 1941. The isolationists called us 'war-mongers' as a term of abuse. We made it a term of defiance. We wanted war with Germany, and strove to promote it. We were not content with giving or selling arms to our friends in order that they might die in our defence. I was involved in most of the war-mongering, so here I can speak from experience. Otherwise, except for anecdotes from my

occasional trips to the lonely island, I rely on the books and
the unpublished diaries and papers which are listed in my
bibliography.

An often-quoted comment of Admiral Mahan on the British
fleet at the height of Napoleon's wars was: 'Those far-distant
storm-beaten ships, upon which the Grand Army never looked,
stood between it and the dominion of the world.' (There are
so many more people in the world since Napoleon's day that
I doubt whether Hitler wanted more than Europe plus North
and South America.) I hope to remind all of us how Great
Britain, this near-by storm-beaten island upon which Hitler
never looked, stood between him and the dominion of the
West.

If the last sentence sounds exaggerated, for those who were
not adult or were not born at the time, I quote Winston
Churchill to his Ambassador in Washington (June 9, 1940):
'If Britain broke under invasion, a pro-German Government
might obtain far easier terms from Germany by surrendering
the fleet, thus making Germany and Japan master of the New
World.'

This was not an attempt to make President Roosevelt's flesh
creep. Had the British given in the Germans would have
found sufficient local Quislings to do their dirty work. Such
people appear when the going gets rough. General de Gaulle,
who arrived in London eight days after that message from
Churchill, writes in his *Memoirs:* 'But the well-informed whis-
pered the names of politicians, bishops, writers and business-
men who . . . would come to terms with the Germans to assure
. . . the administration of the country.'

The United States had a one-ocean Fleet, most of which
had just been moved to the Pacific. The Germans would have
gobbled up the French Fleet if they conquered Britain. Who
would then have stopped Hitler in the West, Japan in the
East? In those innocent days before the Bomb, the command
of the oceans was the command which must be obeyed. Pos-

sibly not by Russia; but Hitler could have dealt with Russia in a one-front war had not the British been obdurate.

In a vague way, most people know these facts, even the young; but most people, especially the young, have forgotten what the world would be like had the Nazis won. If we remind ourselves, as I hope to do, of this one great truth of recent history we shall not only remember our debt to Britain but we may become less discontented with the world of today. With all our frustrations and iniquities we live in an earthly paradise compared to what the Nazis had planned.

As early as May 15, 1933, the great Thomas Mann, with his novelist's flair for human iniquity, wrote to Einstein: 'It is my deepest conviction that this whole "German Revolution" is wrong and evil . . . in its essence it is not a "rising", no matter how its proponents rant on, but a terrible falling into hatred, vengeance, lust for killing . . . I shall never believe that any good can come of it, either for Germany or the world.' This was written only a few weeks after Hitler came to power. Had its prescience been more widely shared there would be no point to this book.

2

Long, long ago a professor who had taken his doctorate in history at the Sorbonne was trying to teach me Old French. I asked him whether the Sorbonne really expected a man to spend several years on the history of a single year. He answered indirectly: 'So much more happens in a year than in a century. You can skip through a century with a few hundred books, chronicles, collections of documents; but if you start on one year, any year, there is no limit to how much you must learn.'

Most of my professors when I was taking my own doctorate had been trained in Germany. They taught me that the writing of contemporary history was certainly useless and probably sinful, involving a betrayal of scholarship. Lord Acton's timeless impartiality was their ideal: wait until all the documents are available (they never are) and then write as if you sat on the horn of the moon without country, background, personality or linguistic problems.

Thus was I taught. And now in my old age I am trying to recreate the deeds and passions of a contemporary terror. Nobody can say I was not warned, or that I have not warned my readers.

Another warning: I said I speak from experience on American war-time politics; but experience is not knowledge. My friends and I tried to push the United States into war long before Pearl Harbor. We failed; but we were useful here and there and we learned a lot. When writing about this I am not even writing contemporary history. I am writing personal memoirs which might be useful to some historian some day—but only when he can compare them with many other memories.

Herbert Agar,
  Beechwood,
    Petworth,
      Sussex.

I
Background to War

1

France had fallen on June 22, 1940, and on July 19 Hitler made
the last of his 'final' peace-offers to Britain. When this had been
rejected by the Government and laughed at by the people,
The Times of London reprinted this from the *New York
Times:*

'Hitler has spoken and Lord Halifax has answered. There
is no more to be said. Or is there? Is the tongue of Chaucer,
of Shakespeare, of the King James translation of the Scriptures,
of Keats, of Shelley, to be hereafter, in the British Isles, the
dialect of an enslaved race? . . .

'From our own shores we cannot see the shadow over ancient gardens, over houses hoary with age, over the graves
of poets and philosophers, and the tombs of the martyrs. We
know only that one of the green and lovely oases of civilization
in the wilderness of man's time on earth is foully threatened,
and that the whole world forever more will be the poorer if
it falls.'

This was the mood of the West. People everywhere were
watching breathlessly, unable to believe that England could
resist, unable to believe that England could fall. We only knew
that if she fell it would be in battle and not at a conference.

What had brought our world to this pass? Why the war and

why the collapse of France? These questions must be answered before we can 'feel' Britain's lonely year.

Why the war? Already I have offended some historians by saying in my Preface that Britain saved the West. I shall continue to offend the same people since I believe that Hitler went to war by design and not by accident, and that Nazi Germany was at least as brutal as we thought in 1940. The more we learn, the more unworthy seem the Nazis to whom the German people abdicated all power during the 1930s. Churchill wrote, with his graceful ferocity, that Hitler 'called from the depths of defeat the dark and savage furies latent in the most numerous, most serviceable, ruthless, contradictory and ill-starred race in Europe'. I suggest that the magic of Hitler was stranger than this. He called from the depths a group of jealous buffoons who hated each other, who crawled before their Fuehrer, and who shared the one talent of mesmerising that 'ill-starred race'.

2

After each war with Germany we have revisionist historians who insist that the war was not at all the way it seemed to those of us who were in it, and that we were wrong to think that we had been fighting for a worthy cause. After the Kaiser-war these historians depraved the minds of many Americans, creating the isolationism which was almost fatal in 1940. Strangely, although the results of the Second World War were even more disappointing than those of the First, the American revisionists have now entangled themselves in an effort to show that the whole thing was the fault of President Roosevelt. This has got them nowhere. As Professor Ferrell notes: 'Despite the altogether disquieting aftermath of the war, most Americans still believe that it was necessary to suppress by force the aggressive régimes in Berlin and Tokyo.'

In England, however, important writers are now suggesting that Hitler blundered into war almost by accident, certainly not by deep design, and that he was driven into the stance of a modern Napoleon by the stupidities of the Allies. This, I suggest, underestimates Hitler's guilt and exaggerates the faults of the unhappy 'men of Munich'.

The question is simple: Am I right in believing that the rough outline and the major aims of the six-years-war are to be found in *Mein Kampf* and thus were long-contemplated? A. J. P. Taylor says 'No'. He denies that Hitler had always planned to ruin France and to make Germany lord of the Continent. In his exhilarating book, *The Origins of the Second World War*, he dismisses the threats in *Mein Kampf* as an emotional reaction to the French occupation of the Ruhr. He admits that Hitler intended to make Germans a great power in Western Europe and to gain *Lebensraum* from Russia in the East. The *Lebensraum* he agrees, must not be over-crowded; so where do the Russians go?

Hitler, says Mr Taylor, thought these good things could fall into his lap without a great war, through the folly of other people—although big threats and little wars might be needed. He had become head of the German State not by careful planning but because foolish people put him at the top intending to use him.

'Far from wanting war', writes Mr Taylor, 'a general war was the last thing [Hitler] wanted. He wanted the fruits of total victory without total war; and thanks to the stupidity of others he nearly got them.' So the broken victims of Nazi aggression must be blamed for their agony on the grounds of their longing for peace. Liddell Hart carries this complicated argument still further in his *History of the Second World War*. Here the Germans almost became the dupes of Chamberlain and Halifax.

'How, then,' asks Liddell Hart, 'did it come about that [Hitler] became involved in the major war that he had been so anxious to avoid?' The answer is to be found not merely, nor most, in Hitler's aggressiveness, but in the encouragement

he had long received from the complaisant attitude of the
Western Powers coupled with their sudden turn-about in the
spring of 1939. 'That reversal [i.e. the guarantee to Poland]
was so abrupt and unexpected as to make war inevitable . . .
The Polish guarantee was the surest way to produce an early
explosion, and a world war.'

Liddell Hart points out that the British Government had
allowed (perhaps encouraged) Hitler to believe that his search
for *Lebensraum* to the East need not lead to war with
the West. Also, in September 1938 the British and French Governments had turned down a Russian offer to join in the defence of Czechoslovakia, thus appearing to dismiss Eastern
Europe as of small account. So Hitler felt betrayed when the
decision to 'support' Poland was announced. 'I'll cook them a
stew that they'll choke on,' he shouted.

Nevertheless, no matter how much we blame the Western
Powers for their maundering (and the United States for selfish
folly about reparations and war debts), Hitler had a consistent
purpose which he had laid down in *Mein Kampf* fourteen
years before he went to war and at least sixteen years before
he began to go daft. The timing he left to the Fates (or their
Nordic equivalent); but the plan was exact: the 'betrayed
Germans' in Austria, Czechoslovakia and Poland must first
be rescued; then France must go, leaving England confused
and ineffective; then Russia.

Obviously, Hitler hoped to do all this on the quiet, or with
a few small wars; but if it meant the big war, he was content
to take the chance when the hour was ripe. Liddell Hart is
mistaken in thinking that the abrupt promise to Poland was a
light-minded caprice. Militarily, it may have been ridiculous;
but morally the guarantee (or something equally dramatic)
had become necessary. The British people and their Government had seen at last that European civilisation was at stake,
that Hitler and his shabby court had to be challenged. The
Polish guarantee defeated nobody except the Poles; but it called
a halt. It announced that the British, who are slow to wrath,

admitted that their efforts to assuage the unassuageable had failed.

Ian Colvin, the *News Chronicle* correspondent in Berlin, may have influenced the choice of Poland as the place to make a stand. Late in March 1939 he told Lord Halifax that Poland was positively the next country on Hitler's list. He added that if Britain gave clear proof that she would fight for Poland the German General Staff might call a halt to their all-aspiring Fuehrer. Like other rumours of serious resistance in Germany, this proved false; but Chamberlain made his guarantee to Poland two days after Mr Colvin's report, on March 31. He may have dreamed that the German generals would play their part and that even militarily his promise would not prove vain. Hope died slowly (first in Britain, and later in the United States) among those who thought that the Nazis could be dealt with like normal human beings.

The *Diaries* of Sir Alexander Cadogan offer a more sophisticated view of the promise to Poland:

Our guarantee could give no possible protection to Poland in any immediate attack . . . But it set up a signpost for himself [Chamberlain]. He was committed, and in the event of a German attack on Poland he would be spared the agonising doubts and indecisions. Our military situation must have been known to them and they should have been aware of the imminence of the peril that threatened them. You may say that it was cynical. On a short view perhaps it was. But it *did* bring us into the war . . . The poor Poles cannot be expected to appreciate the result for them.

Surely not. Cadogan seems to be suggesting that the Poles had to die in order to help Chamberlain clear his muddled mind. This sounds unfair both ways.

According to Albert Speer, Hitler always wanted to go to war over Poland and intended to provoke battle no matter how humbly the Allies might cringe. Speer quotes the Fuehrer:

'Do you think it would have been good fortune for our troops if we had taken Poland without a fight, after obtaining Austria

and Czechoslovakia without fighting? Believe me, not even the
best army can stand that sort of thing. Victories without loss
of blood are demoralising. Therefore it was not only fortunate
there was no compromise; at the time we would have had to
regard it as harmful, and I therefore would have struck in
any case.'

Speer, the self-styled parent of German arms-production,
is not the best witness when it comes to his own doings; but
he was the nearest thing to a friend Hitler ever found. And
he was in and out of Hitler's house—wherever that mobile unit
might appear—more than any other man. Thus I am inclined
to believe his tale which, if true, does not suggest a Hitler eager above all else to avoid a big war.

And I find unsympathetic the theory that the proximate
cause of the war was the dithering of Chamberlain, Halifax,
Daladier and Co. I see nothing base or stupid in these last,
sad efforts to treat Germany as if she were sane. Granted that
Chamberlain distrusted France, hated Russia and hoped for
friendship with Germany; those who write off his policy as a
silly result of these silly opinions forget some of the 'information' which the Government had at the time and which could
neither be ignored nor appraised.

Baldwin, who knew nothing about aviation, had announced
that 'the bomber will always get through' and Kingsley Martin
of the *New Statesman*, who normally thought Baldwin a joke,
believed this nonsense faithfully. Then Baldwin resigned in
May 1937, just in time to avoid the fatal decisions. Neville
Chamberlain, who succeeded, was shocked by the first report
from the Committee of Imperial Defence. The Committee
warned him that a German air attack on London lasting sixty
days would kill 600,000 people and injure twice that number.
This was indeed a pretty dish to set before the new Prime
Minister.

Furthermore, everyone had for years been quoting figures
from the Italian General Douhet's book of horrors. A city,

said Douhet, could be destroyed by bombers in a day: then 'ten, twenty, fifty cities . . . A complete breakdown of the social structure cannot but take place in a country subjected to this kind of merciless pounding from the air . . . The disintegrations of nations . . . will be achieved by aerial forces.'

In fact, after five and a half years of aerial warfare, after the Blitz and all the other horrors, a little more than 60,000 people were killed by bombing throughout the whole of the British Isles. The discrepancy is so amazing that it recalls what the navy could do in the way of false estimates. At the time of the Abyssinian crisis, the Government was told by its naval advisers that the British Mediterranean Fleet, plus the entire Home Fleet, could not cope with the Italian navy and air force. Later, with the British navy engaged world-wide, Admiral Cunningham disposed of the Italians with a shadow of these forces.

During the First World War the Germans had invented 'strategic bombing', or 'total air warfare', or the bombing of civilians, as an indiscriminate form of terror. The British responded as soon as they had the necessary de Havilland 4s for which Lord Trenchard had been begging. A new device for seeking to compel submission can never be left to one camp only. During those first days of air warfare, the Germans dropped about 300 tons of bombs on the British Isles, causing 4,820 casualties, including 1,430 dead. Thus came the guess that in the next war 'in densely populated areas such as London, there will be fifty casualties per ton of bomb dropped. Of these casualties, one-third will be killed and two-thirds wounded.'

And how many tons could London expect each night? By 1937 the Air Staff estimated that within two years the Germans could average some 644 per twenty-four hours, adding that since the Germans liked to be as *schrecklich* as possible they might start with 3,500 tons during the first twenty-four hours. Fifty times 3,500 gives 175,000 casualties, among whom a little more than 58,000 should be dead. And this on the first day, according to the best (or at any rate the only) advice.

How many light-hearted condemners of 'appeasement' have tried to think themselves into 10 Downing Street at dawn, in the weakest hour of the spirit, faced with these so-called facts? What would you or I do about the 600,000 dead, or even about the 58,000 which should already have perished if the war began yesterday? Would we think it wrong to try again, in the hope that Hitler might not be implacable?

Chamberlain believed in facts, like any Lord Mayor of Birmingham, and 'facts' were served to him. Churchill thought facts were cranky and demanded miracles and saved the world; but if Hitler had been a little more normal Chamberlain might have saved thirty million lives plus a world-wide civil war plus the hydrogen bomb which still may prove at any hour that man is a failed experiment. Who knows? Who would like to have made Chamberlain's decisions? By the time Churchill had inherited, the war was well on its way and there were none of these problems: only victory or death.

Adding fortuitously to the indecisions and the torture of Chamberlain, General Vuillemin (Chief of Staff of the French air army) visited Germany for a week in August 1938 as Goering's guest. Vuillemin convinced himself that the Germans had nothing but friendly feelings toward France, and his hosts convinced him that the Luftwaffe and the airplane industry of Germany were unsurpassably powerful and efficient. He told François-Poncet, his Ambassador in Berlin, that the French air force would not last a fortnight against the Germans. Then he carried the news to Paris, whence it was relayed to London on the eve of Munich.

Another prophet of woe, another nuisance to Chamberlain, was Charles Lindbergh, fresh from his talks with Goering and Messerschmitt. This was the American who had flown a single-engined plane from New York to Paris, and who, oddly, was regarded as an impartial authority on the world's air forces. As for his authority, we shall see he was wrong on every count.

As for his impartiality, three weeks after Munich he was awarded, and accepted, the 'Service Cross of the German Eagle with Star'.[1] Such was the man who undertook, in the late 1930s, to intimidate the British and the French and, incidentally, the Americans.

As a sample of what Lindbergh was saying he told Tom Jones,[2] who recorded it in his *Diary*, that the air power of Germany was greater than that of all the European nations (including Russia, whose strength he derided) and that the Germans 'could not be prevented by us or by France from laying the great capitals level with the ground . . . Since my talk with Lindbergh, I've sided with those working for peace, at any cost and any humiliation, because of the picture of our relative unpreparedness in the air and on the ground which Lindbergh painted, and because of his belief that the democracies would be crushed absolutely and finally.'

The Germans had no such power as Lindbergh suggested. Why did the British Government listen to him? The Committee of Imperial Defence, yes; it must be respected. The head of the French air force, yes. But why Lindbergh? He had taken refuge in England after his son was murdered in New Jersey and he did not even sense the imperturbable pugnacity of his mild-mannered hosts. He went on predicting Great Britain's defeat until the day America was brought into the war. His judgment on Hitler was equally odd. In the spring of 1939 he recorded in his *Wartime Journals:* 'It seems to me that this man, damned almost everywhere except in his own country, called a fanatic and a madman, now holds the future of Europe in his hand. Civilisation depends upon his wisdom far more than on the action of the democracies.'

Lindbergh was believed. He had youthful charm plus the maximum of physical daring. He added more than any other civilian to the French and British fear that war against Hitler

[1] A decoration conferred upon foreigners who 'deserved well of the Reich'.

[2] Deputy Secretary of the Cabinet, 1917–1930, etc.

meant national suicide. And he was right had the Nazis won; but he proved a misery in his underestimate of the British. Albert Speer, after 1942 the minister for production, writes:

'The obverse of Hitler's claim to world leadership was the subjugation of nations. I knew that France was to be relegated to satellite status, that Belgium and Holland and even Burgundy were to be incorporated into Hitler's Reich: I knew that the Poles and Russians were to be extinguished as nations and turned into serf peoples. Moreover, for him who wished to hear, Hitler had made no secret of his intention to exterminate the Jewish people.'

This was written later, but it is not the description of a man who hoped to change the world by persuasion and by the folly of his neighbours.

We may never know how to come to terms with Hitler's tenebrous mind. Alan Bullock, I feel, has made the wisest exploration of that secret place. He says there are two views of Hitler's foreign policy, 'the fanatic and the opportunist'. The first stresses mad racialism and the insistence from early days that Germany must conquer *Lebensraum* in Eastern Europe at the cost of the sub-human Slavs and the nonhuman Jews.[3] The second view dismisses all this (and the whole of *Mein Kampf*) as fantasy-life, and stresses Hitler's opportunism. He never had a timetable, either in becoming Chancellor or in launching his aggressions. He waited for things to come his way, for the fruit to fall into his lap. And it often did.

Mr Bullock says that we should not 'treat these two contrasting views as alternatives, for if that is done, then whichever alternative is adopted, a great deal of evidence has to be ignored'. Hitler, Mr Bullock believes, was both fanatic and opportunist: '. . . convinced of his role as man of destiny *and* prepared to use all the actor's arts in playing it . . . Consistency of aim with complete opportunism in method and tactics.

[3] Strictly, the word Slav should be confined to philology; but Hitler was not careful in his usage.

This is, after all, a classical receipt for success in foreign affairs.'

The full industrial resources of Germany were not used for rearmament even after the war began—a fact which has been used to suggest that Hitler did not intend war. The truth I think, is that he intended exactly what he got, up to 1941: a series of *blitzkriegs* carried out by troops trained and equipped for brief, stabbing, lethal attacks. Had Britain either fallen or made peace, these 'short, decisive blows', as Hitler called them, could have made him master of the Western World. Alan Bullock lists the blows: 'Poland, four weeks; Norway, two months; Holland five days, Belgium seventeen days; France six weeks; Yugoslavia, eleven days; Greece, three weeks.' And Mr Bullock adds: 'The explanation of why the German army was allowed to invade Russia without winter clothing or equipment is Hitler's belief that even Russia could be knocked out by a *blitzkrieg* in four or five months, before winter set in.'

The belief might have come true had it not been for the stubborn British.

At times, Liddell Hart in his last book seems to resent this stubbornness which upset so many careful German plans. He seems to feel that if the men and women of Britain had known their military history they would have surrendered meekly after the fall of France.

Alan Bullock sums up his lecture, *Hitler and the Origins of the Second World War:* 'Not only did Hitler create the threat of war and exploit it, but when it came to the point he was prepared to take the risk and go to war, and then when he had won the Polish campaign, to redouble the stakes and attack again, first in the West, then in the East.'

This was the meaning of Nazism: conquest. In July 1941, in Alsace, the Administrative President for the Third Reich announced: 'Providence has placed the German people at the very heart of Europe and has entrusted us with the mission of establishing order in Europe. We shall wrest from those peoples who live in our *Lebensraum* such areas as we need to accommodate and feed not only ourselves but our

posterity: namely 200 million Germans. And we shall drive
out of these areas all the heterogeneous peoples.' These are
not the words of a government that has been driven reluc-
tantly into war by the dithering of its neighbours.

Returning to my question: is it right to condemn the Nazis
as killers and to impute to Hitler an implacable thrust toward
conquest? I think the answer is 'yes' and that it is important
to establish the 'yes' (when writing about Hitler's war) before
revisionist historians confuse the issue beyond hope. I also
think that the pre-war rulers of Great Britain and France, in
view of the 'facts' presented to them, deserve some pity for
their efforts to cling to peace. The failure to rearm mightily
seems in retrospect their greatest fault; but anyone who lived
in England at the time has a right to ask, 'Who was prepared to
vote the Government the money?'

During the grisly last days at Bordeaux, with France pros-
trate, Reynaud turned on Weygand, who was insisting on an
armistice. 'You take Hitler for William I,' said Reynaud, 'an
old gentleman who took Alsace-Lorraine from us and left it
at that. But Hitler is Genghis Khan!' This was the whole point
of the war. This is why the revisionist historians are wrong.
This is why the British had to fight, not only alone, but even
if they were beaten in their own island, even if a few men and
children from the Hebrides had to represent what once was
Europe in Canada or in the South Pacific.

On May 21, 1940, when the Germans had reached the
Channel ports, Oliver Harvey (Minister at the British Embassy in Paris) wrote to a friend: 'My God! what a pass those
bloody old men have brought us to! We were never ruthless
enough with them I'm afraid. What a responsibility both S.B.
and Neville bear . . . !' This was a fair reaction during that
shattering week, especially for a friend of Anthony Eden. Yet
we shall see that it was not the 'old men', for all their slowness
and delusions, who were responsible for the Germans reaching
Abbeville. That was the work of the French generals, to whom
the British perhaps inevitably submitted.

II
The Loss of France

1

Professor Guy Chapman rightly says that 'the defeat of France in 1940 began twenty years earlier . . . In the year 1919 the French were battered, worn, plundered and frustrated'. Almost 1,400,000 Frenchmen had been killed in the war and another 740,000 were mutilated, many of them useless to themselves as well as to France; and 3,000,000 were wounded.

'Plundered' is an accurate word in Professor Chapman's lament. Ten Departments, most of them the centres of French industry, had been fought over and largely destroyed. Factories and mines had been sabotaged and robbed of their machinery. Towns and villages had been eradicated, along with many of the villagers and all the farm animals. Neither Germany nor England had been 'plundered'.

Professor Chapman's key word is 'frustrated'. Worse than the ruin of the country, worse than all the dead men, was the peace; the betrayal of France's security by the United States primarily, and to a lesser extent by Great Britain. Security, now to be denied them by their friends, is why all those Frenchmen died. And France had paid more than her share for victory. In January, 1918, before the Americans had appeared seriously, the Belgians had twelve divisions in the field; the British had sixty-one divisions and the French ninety-nine divisions.

When it came to 'peace-making', the minority (in terms of troops) would not let the majority protect itself. On the four main points at issue: frontiers, guarantees for the future, reparations and war debts, France was done down. The blame lay largely with the newcomer, the United States.

Foch wanted the Rhine as France's frontier with Germany. This alone would bring safety to France, Belgium and the Western World. Clemenceau agreed; but he found it was politically impossible. The Americans and the British—at what then seemed a safe distance from Berlin—were mollifying their distaste for Germans, and men like Maynard Keynes were already warning against inhumanity to these people.

At the Peace Conference Clemenceau used the Rhine frontier as a bargaining point, in the hope of some other concession to French safety. The British proposed that they and the Americans should each, simultaneously, guarantee to support France if she were again attacked by Germany. President Wilson agreed. The British Parliament agreed. The American Senate flatly refused.

A 'simultaneous' guarantee by one nation is implausible so the whole matter was dropped and France was left without a strong frontier and without promise of support for the next time the German volcano erupted. Few allies have been betrayed so quickly or so sanctimoniously. 'Defeat substituted for victory, that was what we accepted,' wrote Clemenceau. 'It is not a peace treaty,' said Foch, 'it is a twenty-year armistice.' 'Isolated and deceived and deserted' was the feeling of France, according to Churchill.

Years later Pétain recalled that he had wept on the evening of the 'premature' armistice, wept for the million and a half dead soldiers of France who deserved a victory worthy of their sacrifice. Without the Rhine frontier there could be no such victory. And without the invasion of Germany and the total defeat of her armies, he foresaw that there would be no Rhine frontier.

Or, as Napoleon said: *Vaincre n'est rien: il faut profiter du succès.*

The Treaty of Versailles (Articles 231–246) declared Germany's obligation to repair in full the material losses she had inflicted upon persons and property. The British and the Americans wanted to name a fixed sum. Clemenceau insisted that 'it is impossible to attempt to fix the cost of reparations if we do not wish to delay the conclusion of the Treaty indefinitely'. When Clemenceau won the argument, Keynes resigned as adviser to the British Delegation and wrote *The Economic Consequences of the Peace.* The book taught that the Treaty was morally and economically wrong. The prosperity of Europe and of the world, said Keynes, was tied to the prosperity of Germany. Germany should not be asked to pay too much. This suited the growing tenderness about Germany in Britain and the United States. Then Germany abruptly made clear that she had no intention of paying 'too much' and that she alone would settle the meaning of those ambiguous words.

In 1921 the Reparations Articles of the Treaty were abandoned in favour of a fixed sum: 132,000 million gold marks. France was to receive about 68,000 million[1]—rather less than half the estimate of the physical destruction in France.

When expressed in terms of cash, the plan looks ridiculous; nobody could produce cash on such a scale. When put in terms of machinery, cows and cottages, reparations seem less foolish. Had there been the will, Germany might have paid a fair amount in goods and services; but there was no will, and by 1921 no nation was prepared (or perhaps able) to enforce the Treaty. When Poincaré, by occupying the Ruhr, tried to make Germany give at least a token sum of reparations the world denounced him as a tyrant. Perhaps reparations were unrealistic. The French people did not think so. They were told to expect reparations and they felt swindled. They also felt that their recent friends condoned the swindle.

[1] The average sterling value of the mark through 1921 was 408 to the £.

The proper policy toward Germany, many have said, was to help her grow prosperous and to prevent her from rearming. The implication is that the Allies and the United States did the opposite. Yet Germany received large private loans from the United States, plus smaller loans from Great Britain, plus millions of dollars from deluded Americans who bought marks 'because they must go up'. Germany then devalued the mark to zero, trapping the dollars and freeing herself from internal debt. The fact that she incidentally ruined her middle-class paved the way for Hitler. German policy—not British, French or American policy—paved the way for Hitler. And as for preventing German rearmament, nobody could (or would) do that once the United States had denied the League of Nations and betrayed collective security.

A. J. P. Taylor puts the long bewilderment of reparations succinctly: 'No doubt the apprehensions of Keynes and the Germans were grotesquely exaggerated. No doubt the impoverishment of Germany was caused by war, not by reparations . . . In actual fact, as everyone now knows, Germany was a net gainer by the financial transactions of the nineteen-twenties: she borrowed far more from private American investors (and failed to pay back) than she paid in reparations.' And Professor Taylor points out that the facts about reparations were of small importance. Reparations had become a symbol. They bred hatred and suspicion among 'the Allied and Associated powers'. And in Germany they were an excuse for every malfeasance. A British statesman had talked of squeezing the German orange till the pips squeaked; yet soon the British were accusing the French of inhumanity because they wanted some of their dead animals and ruined factories replaced. The Germans learned to whine about the 'slave treaty' of Versailles from the British and the Americans who had helped concoct the Treaty and whose Prime Minister, and whose President, had signed it.

'More than anything else', wrote Professor Taylor, 'they [reparations] cleared the way for the Second World War.' And

the Second World War showed the folly of the soft talk about
a Germany impoverished by reparations. Stalin, twenty-one
years later, said he did not want money; he wanted goods.
'Germany should pay reparation in kind.' So the Russians took
everything that was movable from their zone. Germany was
laid flat, and then partitioned. And in no time West Germany
was richer than she had ever been. And still the textbooks repeat that Germany's troubles between the wars stemmed from
the Treaty of Versailles. And some people may believe it.

Just after the signing of the Treaty Monsieur Klotz, Minister
of Finance, encouraged the French people to hope they would
really get reparations. Marshal Foch blasted him: *'Monsieur le
Ministre,* . . . *avec un pareil traité, vous pourrez vous
présenter aux guichets de l'empire allemand, et vous serez
payé—en monnaie de singe.'* 'Monkey money' is a good name
for what the French got out of Germany.

For France, the final, painful turn of the screw came when
the United States insisted on full payment of her war loans
to the Allies, meanwhile raising her tariffs so that payment
became impossible. This folly is explicable. During the First
World War the United States, who had long been heavily in
debt to the outside world, became the greatest creditor nation
of modern times; but she did not learn the first lesson of the
creditor nation: in order to be paid she must encourage a brisk
trade with her debtors. President Coolidge's bit of nonsense,
'They hired the money didn't they?', was as stupid a comment
as possible. They did not hire money. They hired guns and
ammunition and airplanes and shipping and lorries. Had they
been allowed to sell to America, after the war, large quantities
of the peace-time equivalent of such goods they could have
paid their debts and half-solved their problem of unemployment. The ever-rising American tariffs forbade.

Since America did not want to be paid, did not want the
goods and services from abroad, why make a fuss about non-
payment? Perhaps the American trade unions and politicians
were right in rejecting foreign goods. They could not have

been right in abusing the foreigners whose goods were refused.

Until startled into a fitful thoughtfulness by the fall of France, the United States was not a useful member of the international community. She often seemed on the point of doing something wise; but nothing happened. For example:

(1) The Lausanne Conference (June–July, 1932) cut German reparations to almost nothing on the assumption of an American reduction in war debts. America refused. So by 1934 Germany had repudiated reparations and every country except Finland had defaulted on its war debts.[2] France and Britain were bitterly blamed by Americans for repudiating debts. Germany was scarcely blamed for repudiating reparations.

(2) When Hitler became Chancellor in 1933, few Americans took the trouble to notice his distaste for the United States. 'Transplant a German to Kiev', he complained, 'and he remains a perfect German. But transplant him to Miami, and you make a degenerate of him—in other words, an American.' This was a sound grievance. The Nazi racial theories become a joke when faced by an Eisenhower or a Carl Schurz. Germany has enriched America and impoverished herself. In *Mein Kampf* Hitler takes a different view. America, he says, is debauched by German Jews. 'Only one great man, Ford' kept the Jews from winning without opposition from the cringing goyim. 'America', he said later, 'is permanently on the brink of revolution. It will be a simple matter for me to produce unrest and revolt in the United States . . . Our strategy is to destroy the enemy from within.' And on November 12, 1940, Ribbentrop told an unresponsive Molotov: 'The entry of the United States into the war is of no consequence at all for Germany.' Germany, he added, would never again allow an Anglo-Saxon to land on the European Continent. Luckily for us, our enemies can also be silly.

2 Finland did not suffer from the American tariff-system because her forests were needed in America for newsprint. This seemed a classic case for Lesson One in economics. Yet nobody could persuade the inert masses that 'gallant little Finland' paid her debts because she was allowed to, whereas richer countries did not because they were not allowed to.

France was doubly discouraged when America seemed immune to the truth about Hitler, seemed to be living in a world which had no relation to the fate of anybody, including herself.

(3) Norman Davis was sent to Europe by President Roosevelt in the spring of 1933 to report on many problems. He met Hitler on May 8 and concluded that France had no reason to fear Germany but that Germany must have equality in arms. He added that 'Hitler's moderate attitude was somewhat encouraging'. The President, luckily, was not encouraged. He asked Congress for a law which would allow him to embargo arms and ammunition to any country that threatened or committed aggression. Congress refused, unless the embargo applied to all nations in a dispute, not merely to the aggressor. The matter was dropped. Thus perished the last chance of effective American aid to collective security. Hitler took note, and so did the frustrated and the defeatists in France.

Despondent Frenchmen must have felt justified by rumours of the behaviour of the American Ambassador at the Court of St James's. (We now know that the rumours were true.) Joseph Kennedy believed that if he could talk with Hitler the two of them would solve the problems of peace. He asked the German Ambassador (Herbert von Dirksen) for an invitation to Berlin. He apologised for the attitude toward Germany of some members of the Administration (notably Harold Ickes, Secretary of the Interior), ascribing it to the influence of Jews in eastern America. He told the Ambassador that of course Germany should have colonies and a free hand economically in eastern and southern Europe. He said he was 'prepared to support Germany's demands *vis-à-vis* England or to do anything that might lead to a pacification'. Two weeks after Munich he asked for a conference with Hitler. The conference never took place; but the alleged views of the American Ambassador were discussed by journalists and politicians in every capital in Europe and they gave heart to the type of

Frenchman who was already murmuring 'better Hitler than Blum'.

This Ambassador is not given credit for the harm he did, the fear he spread. As soon as the war began he asked King George VI: how could Britain win, and was not the cost too dreadful? He got a stiff answer: 'Misery and suffering of war we know . . . The British Empire's mind is made up. I leave it at that.' Undeterred, Kennedy warned his friends in Boston two months later: 'Don't let anything that comes out of any country in the world make you believe that you can make the situation one whit better by getting into the war. There is no place in this fight for us.' Such talk did not encourage the Allies, during May and June, 1940, when their best hope was help from America.

According to the Morgenthau Diaries, Roosevelt agreed with my friends. As early as October 1939, the President complained that Kennedy 'has always been an appeaser and always will be an appeaser . . . He's just a pain in the neck to me.'

2

I have discussed these between-the-wars problems from the French point of view, which is the only one that counts if we wish to understand France's state of mind in 1940.

The German point of view was stated by Keynes as early as 1919 and was later embellished by Hitler. 'The nature of the contract between Germany and the Allies is plain and unequivocal,' wrote Keynes; 'the terms of the peace are to be in accordance with the Addresses of the President [Wilson], and the purpose of the Conference is "to discuss the details of their application". The circumstances of the contract were of an unusually solemn and binding character; for one of the conditions of it was that Germany was to agree to Armistice terms which were to be such as to leave her helpless. Germany having rendered herself helpless in reliance on the contract, the honour of the Allies was peculiarly involved in fulfilling their part.'

This is specious. Germany had not 'rendered herself helpless' because of Woodrow Wilson's speeches. She had been rendered helpless by the armies of France and Great Britain. And she had been rendered hopeless by the gathering might of the United States. Helpless and hopeless, she grasped at the Wilsonian rhetoric; yet it is doubtful whether anybody but Keynes (until Hitler strode upon the stage) believed that Germany had been 'tricked' into an armistice when she might have gone on fighting. On the contrary, the Allies were tricked into restraining Foch from invading the Fatherland—as he could have done, and should have done, and as Pétain (Commander-in-Chief of the French armies) wished to do.

Yet Keynes insisted, to the applause of the disillusioned and the rebellious, that at the Peace Conference 'two rival schemes for the future policy of the world took the field—the Fourteen Points of the President, and the Carthaginian Peace of M. Clemenceau. Yet only one of these was entitled to take the field: for the enemy had not surrendered unconditionally, but on agreed terms as to the general character of the peace.'

This is worse than specious; it is naïve. When the Germans in their despair, and in their astonishment at defeat, grasped at the Fourteen Points, they knew that anything was better than another month of war. Hence the armistice. The surprising thing about the subsequent Peace Treaty is that it did pay some heed to the Fourteen Points.

Who can blame Foch for his fury and despair over the Treaty? Wars are horrible; soldiers know this better than civilians; but if you win a war you expect a small prize to set against your dead men. Foch was no dreamer. He did not think the near-suicide of Europe would make the world a better place; but he did think that victory might give France time to renew her farms, her factories and her people. Instead, he got a 'twenty-year armistice'.

If the charitable Fourteen Points had taken the field at the Peace Conference, and held the field, this would have meant that mankind had undergone a sudden moral mutation toward kindliness and friendship (a mutation as far-reaching as geologists once thought could explain the origin of species): an unlikely reward for four years of slaughter. President Wilson, who had never seen anything more grievous than a corrupt politician, may be excused for thinking that the war was fought to make men better; but Keynes had lived in the big world. Why should he have fallen into disillusionment because the war left men exactly as it found them (aside from the millions which it left mutilated or dead)? The peace was bound to be a botched-up compromise between the world-views of Wilson and of Clemenceau: not a useful pair of philosophies to sew together.

Keynes, unfortunately for him and for us, did not know what we now know about the origins of the Kaiser-war. Toward the end of that heart-breaking conflict, many who had watched with a growing horror and incomprehension snatched the vulgar Marxian notion that the war was basically a quarrel over markets: the 'inevitable' quarrel of imperialism leading to the 'inevitable' death of capitalism. We now know better.

We also know, from Professor Fritz Fischer's *Griff nach der Weltmacht*, that there is no truth in the revisionists' theory that the Kaiser's Germany got into the hands of a few wicked expansionists and that Good Germans were opposed. Good Germans, who doubtless existed, were not in the seats of power, nor had they been for a long time. The men who ran Germany—not only the military, but men like the respectable and moderate Bethmann-Hollweg—subscribed to the 'September Programme' of 1914: a Central African Empire carved out of French and British colonies: large, buffer states to the east at the expense of Russia; the annexation of parts of Belgium and France; and the elimination of France as a major power. These are war-aims which Hitler could have signed.

A. J. P. Taylor comments: 'We now know, thanks to Professor Fritz Fischer, what the Germans would have arranged if they had won the First World War. It was a Europe indistinguishable from Hitler's Empire at its greatest extent, including even a Poland and a Ukraine cleared of their native inhabitants.' Such revelations seem to dispose of Keynes's and Hitler's favourite thesis that the War Guilt clause of the Treaty of Versailles was a lie.[3]

Unhappily, the Keynesian view of 'the broken promise' was made to order for Hitler. As one by one he broke the clauses of the Treaty of Versailles, he cried out that the whole thing had been a fraud. And many of the English readers of Keynes felt guilty, wondering whether it was unkind to oppose Hitler. Furthermore, because the quick acceptance of the armistice had prevented the invasion of Germany, Hitler and his like were encouraged to invent 'the stab in the back': their armies had not been defeated; their armies had been betrayed on the home front by Jews and Communists and other scum.

Thus Hitler's speeches were written for him in advance: the faithlessness of the Allies; the betrayal of Germany at Paris and Versailles because she was never invited to 'discuss' the terms of peace but merely handed an ultimatum; the betrayal of Germany at home; the long-suffering and unbeaten German army; reparations; revenge. The script had been prepared by its future victims. Hitler had only to add the anti-semitic bits.

This was not as easy as it sounds. Two 'Jewish problems' were fermenting in Hitler's unsteady mind. The first was 'the conspiracy of world Jewry' as outlined in his favourite forgery, *The Protocols of the Learned Elders of Zion*, concocted in Russia at the turn of the century and brought to Western Europe in 1919. The 'conspiracy', Hitler believed, had defeated Ger-

---

[3] Compare the long article in the *Times Literary Supplement* (of November 12, 1971) on other contemporary German historians who agree with Professor Fischer. I have used only *Griff nach der Weltmacht*.

many in the First World War, had imposed the Treaty of Versailles, the devaluation of the mark and the subsequent poverty. The 'conspiracy' was thus a skilful combination of capitalism and Communism at their worst. In order to deal with this sinister affair he would have to conquer not only Russia but the United States: the October Revolution to the East and the Wall Street to the West.

The second 'Jewish problem' for the Fuehrer was that of the nine million Jews to the east and southeast of the Reich: the Yiddish civilisation. These were real Jews, not hallucinations. Early in 1939 Hitler had promised the Reichstag: 'If the international Jewish financiers inside and outside Europe should again succeed in plunging the nations into a world war, the result will not be the bolshevisation of the earth and thus the victory of Jewry, but the annihilation of the Jewish race throughout Europe.'

Here was the Nazi quandary. The 'Jewish race throughout Europe' was mostly peaceful and poor, living in Galicia and the Russian Pale of Settlement; but the Devil-Jews of Nazi mythology, whose machinations explained all of Germany's troubles, lived—if at all—in the United States and Russia. Perhaps it was a comfort to Hitler to war against both countries and get all his Jews—men, women and ghosts—into the same basket. He killed six million of the real Jews; but his wars on the ghosts killed him.

3

If France's foreign policy and her hopes of protection against Germany had been frustrated by her former allies, her domestic policy was frustrated by herself. Ever since the Revolution, and more so since the Paris Commune of 1871, France has been a divided nation.[4] The extreme republicans see a royalist

---

[4] 'Dès sa naissance,' writes Emmanuel Berl, 'la IIIe République avait paru à la gauche une imposture, et à la droit une forfaiture.'

or a dictator behind every move to strengthen the country;
the extreme right sees the left as little better than a nest of
traitors. Only when France is in danger, and is seen by most
citizens to be in danger, can a temporary union be established.
'The enemy was there to make us friends,' wrote Clemenceau
about the war-days. And he added, 'the enemy is still there.'
Sadly for France and for the world, Clemenceau was one of
the few leaders to remind us, during the delirious twenties,
that 'the enemy is still there'. Clemenceau died in 1929.

'When at Versailles,' he wrote, 'Brockdorff-Rantzau addressed me in the language of the bearer of a challenge, I was
forced to realise that the German revolution was mere
window-dressing, and that, with the aggressor not a whit cured
of his insane folly, we should continue without respite to be
subjected, in a new setting, to the same attack from the same
enemy.' And again, in the last year of his life: 'I pause on the
threshold of the terrible moment when the last great struggle
will be entered upon. Who then shall decide the fate of historic
France, as the fate of Athens, and of Greece itself, was decided
on the day of Chaeronea?'

Clemenceau would have scoffed at the prediction, but when
the 'terrible moment' came the fate of France was decided
by Great Britain, an older foe than Germany. Germany could
not become a menace until she was born, which was only yesterday; but England was as ancient as France. When these
two were brought together by fate in 1914, Kipling wrote:

Where did you refrain from us or we refrain from you?
Ask the wave that has not watched war between us two.

There was no such wave, unless it was frozen solid near one of
the Poles and no use to anyone. Yet if Britain had fallen during her lonely year 'historic France' would have gone the way
of Greek liberties after the victory of Philip of Macedon.

Clemenceau may have read *Mein Kampf* although he does
not quote it. If he had not read it he divined it. His passion

for France protected him from being fooled by Germany; but who else was not fooled? Who among all our leaders had read, and pondered, *Mein Kampf*, which was published in 1925 and 1926? Among Englishmen, I can only suggest Churchill and Duff Cooper.

'France', wrote Hitler, 'is the inexorable mortal enemy of the German people', forever seeking 'a dismembered and shattered Germany'. Thus there must come 'a final active reckoning with France . . . a last decisive struggle . . . only then will we be able to end the eternal, fruitless conflict between ourselves and France'. Elsewhere in the book one learns that Hitler's idea of 'ending a conflict' is ending the people who oppose Germany; slaves or corpses is the choice he offers.

The enslavement of France, *Mein Kampf* makes clear, was the prelude to the plundering of Russia. *Lebensraum* to the East could not be conquered while a free, strong France threatened from the West. Therefore France must go; but *Lebensraum* to the East was Hitler's ultimate goal.

Maynard Keynes wrote, in his description of the Council of Four at Paris in 1919, 'Clemenceau was by far the most eminent member of the Council of Four, and he had taken the measure of his colleagues. He alone both had an idea and had considered it in all its consequences . . . One could not despise Clemenceau or dislike him, but only take a different view as to the nature of civilised man, or indulge, at least, a different hope'.

We all came close to destruction by indulging that 'different hope'. Keynes, as an economist and as a writer, was a commanding figure; but as a forecaster of the European future Keynes has been proved wrong and Clemenceau right. Hopes as to the nature of civilised man, kindness and loans and moratoriums and the abandonment of reparations and abjectness and the most soothing speeches—all these were tried and they were useless.

Ironically, Keynes's *Economic Consequences of the Peace*, which was applauded by the young in the 1920s because it made their elders look silly, became a text-book for the appeasers at the time of Munich. Softness and hopefulness about the Germans had now become an old man's folly. Its practitioners were named 'the Guilty Men' by the new generation of youth. And just as Keynes had given Hitler the theme for his best speeches he now gave Chamberlain an excuse for treating Hitler with sweet reason. Keynes was sadly aware of this, as Kingsley Martin notes in his autobiography and proves through his own correspondence with Keynes.

So the 'final active reckoning with France' was the fated event; but why did nobody tell the French people, even after 1933 when Hitler came to power, or after 1939 when the war began? Clemenceau had complained that 'for the last ten years the French people's rulers have chloroformed them so well, have told them so often that nobody wanted another war and therefore there would not be another, that they have ended by believing it.'

Emerging from their chloroform to find themselves mobilised, lounging uselessly in the Maginot dungeons or on the Belgian frontier, in the midst of the 'phoney war', or *drôle de guerre*, the men asked themselves, 'What is it all about? Is this treason, or war, or merely farce?' The very best, the superb troops who would later be sent vainly into lost Belgium, were suffering drab lives and worrying about who was getting at their girls. No important man in France, no natural leader, told them why they were needed.

They went on muttering about Danzig, which was irrelevant. They were not told to look into 'the fixed, majestic questioning eyes of death': the death of France, who would never again be mother of arts and laws (or even arms) unless they saved her now or someone else saved her later. How many would have faltered had they been told this truth?

None of the French leaders seemed to know about *Mein Kampf*, or even about Spengler, the spiritual godfather of the whole Nazi obsession. And even if the misled troops read English, they would have found little enlightenment outside the

speeches of Winston Churchill and the suspect foreign correspondents in Berlin (suspect, because so many of them told
the truth).

Yet there was one new voice in Great Britain. A few days
after Munich another man who had read Hitler joined
Churchill in reminding the British people what the coming
war must mean. Duff Cooper had resigned as First Lord of
the Admiralty because he could not stomach Munich. While
explaining his resignation to the House of Commons he said
that he was forever being told 'that the people of this country
are not prepared to fight for Czechoslovakia. That was per-
fectly true, but . . . it was not for Czechoslovakia that we
should have been fighting if we had gone to war last week
. . . It was not for the sake of Serbia that we fought in 1914.
It was not even for Belgium, although it occasionally suited
some people to say so. We were fighting then, as we should
have been fighting last week, in order that one Great Power
should not be allowed, in disregard of treaty obligations, of
the laws of nations and the decrees of morality, to dominate
by brutal force the Continent of Europe . . . For that principle
we must ever be prepared to fight'.

Had some Frenchman of equal importance warned his fellow citizens, even as late as 1938, that when war came they
would not be dying for Danzig but for the soul of France,
there might have been more discipline during the *drôle de
guerre.*

> *Lo! thy dread Empire, Chaos! is restored;*
> *Light dies before thy uncreating word.*

The 'uncreating word' was the enemy of France during that
winter of her discontent.

Bravely, Duff Cooper tried to tell his French friends what
they refrained from telling themselves. A few days after his
speech of resignation in the House of Commons he was on
holiday in Paris. He was asked whether he would '*faire une*

conférence' on the world's troubles at the Théâtre des Ambas-
sadeurs. Since the audience had to pay, Duff Cooper doubted
whether there would be one. Yet the theatre was crowded
and he had to give the same *conférence* the next night and to
refuse a third appearance because he was seeking a brief vaca-
tion before returning to a hostile parliament. Surely a native
minister of state, prepared to tell his people the truth, might
have found a similar reception?

Duff Cooper spoke in French. I quote from his own translation: 'All civilisations of which we have knowledge have been
destroyed by man himself . . . The destroyers have always
been inferior to those whom they have destroyed . . . A régime that begins by the public burning of books, which continues by abolishing freedom of thought and speech, which
persecutes religion and which seeks by cruelty to exterminate
an ancient race that gave Christianity to the world amongst
other benefits, is barbarous in the worst meaning of the word
and is the enemy of true civilisation . . . While it is right to
avoid war because we hate it, it is wrong to avoid war because
we fear it'.

Laval and his friends were not among the audiences who
paid to hear such sentiments; nor were the soldiers who waited
for the word which would tell them why they were digging
aimlessly in the frozen mud during the *drôle de guerre*. So
the digging went on, not briskly, between the north end of the
Maginot Line and the Channel; but the boredom and cynicism
grew briskly indeed.

4

Most of us thought at the time that the unnerving period of
the 'phoney war', or *drôle de guerre,* was planned by Hitler to
exploit the boredom and cynicism of the French troops and
the similar boredom of civilians in England. As Lawrence

Thompson in his book *1940* points out, this was the coldest winter in Britain for forty-five years. Thus the long, inexplicable waiting imposed upon British non-combatants 'the petty miseries of burst pipes, a shortage of coal, verminous evacuees and the dim spiritual erosion of the blackout'.

We now know that this was not Hitler's wish but merely his good fortune. When Poland collapsed the Fuehrer made a 'peace offer', rightly regarded as an item for home consumption. Three days later, October 9, he explained to his generals why an immediate offensive to the West was imperative. A long war with France and England would sap Germany's strength and might tempt Russia to attack from the rear. So France must be quickly destroyed. The British would then come to terms. 'The attack', he concluded, 'must be launched this autumn, if conditions are at all possible.'

The generals were not pleased. They tried to persuade Hitler that France could not be downed in a hurry and that he was asking for a long war; yet the date of attack was set for November 12. The weather intervened: boisterous and fiercely cold. Finally a new date was set for January 17. On January 10 a German major, flying through a wicked storm, landed in Belgium with the complete operational plan for the attack. If this was an accident it was the luckiest, and if it was a ruse it was the cleverest, that could possibly have happened. For the plans which were captured were essentially the 1914 plans all over again, with the addition of Holland among the neutrals to be invaded. These plans were taken for truth in Paris and London; just such an invasion were the Allied armies deployed to meet. The deployment, as we shall see, led into a fatal trap.

At this point, after these captured plans, the Belgian Government almost relented and allowed the Allies to take up their defensive line along the Dyle River. Then the weather grew worse. The Germans did not attack. Against the pleas of Admiral of the Fleet Lord Keyes (British liaison officer with the Belgian King) the death-wish, 'neutrality', prevailed and the British and French armies were not allowed into Belgium.

Hitler's continued delay, between January and the invasion of Norway, may have been caused by the weather. Or it may have been caused by the need to invent a wholly new plan for invading France. In any case, the Allies were ready for the old plan, and only for the old plan. The new plan overwhelmed them. Meanwhile the German generals had been given six months to train their troops toward perfection.[5] The French troops, however, loitered the precious months away, losing discipline and losing interest.

As early as November General Sir Alan Brooke attended a parade of Corap's 9th Army: the army that was to break and let the Germans across the Meuse. 'I can still see these troops now,' wrote Sir Alan. 'Seldom have I seen anything more slovenly and badly turned out. Men unshaved, horses ungroomed, clothes and saddlery that did not fit, vehicles dirty, and complete lack of pride in themselves or their units. What shook me most, however, was the look in the men's faces, disgruntled and insubordinate looks, and, although ordered to give "Eyes left", hardly a man bothered to do so. After the ceremony was over Corap invited me to visit some of his defences in the Fôret de St Michel. Here we found a half-constructed and very poor anti-tank ditch with no defences to cover it.'

This is not an angry Briton turning on his Allies ex-post-facto. General Ruby of Huntziger's army complained about the increasing drunkenness among the troops. And General Meny despaired over the indiscipline: 'without permission, secretly at first but soon almost openly, they went away Saturday at midday, sometimes in the morning, to reappear Sunday evening, Monday morning, or even Monday at midday.' A funny sort of army, which was the product of a funny sort of war. And still nobody told these troops, loud enough to be

[5] The High Command had not always been happy at the spirit of the infantry in Poland. When Brauchitsch mentioned this, Hitler had one of the first of his maniacal rages.

heard, that what they were facing was 'a final active reckoning with France . . . a last decisive struggle'. Had they been told, they might have spent those precious months in training, as the Germans were training, rather than in drinking and in stolen weekends. They might have built some adequate defences from Longwy (where the Maginot Line ended) to the Channel. They might even have done whatever Pétain had in mind when he said the Ardennes Forest was impenetrable 'provided we make some special dispositions'. Nobody seemed to know, or to ask, what 'special dispositions' were. In any case, they were not made.

In fairness to the French army we should remember that General Corap's troops were the worst of the lot, and were chosen as such. They were supposed to be defending a safe sector. They believed they had Pétain's word for that. Many splendid armies, worthy of France, were under the listless control of General Gamelin. They fought well. They were not to be blamed for being sent to the wrong places at the wrong time.

Gamelin, with his girlish hands and feet and his prim little mouth, did not look like a war-lord or like the commander of millions of troops. 'Commander' is perhaps the wrong word, for Gamelin mostly sat, without benefit of modern communications, in his cellars at Vincennes while other men carried out his doomed plans. Yet he had made a good reputation in the First World War and he may well have known more military history than any other French general. He did not know how to inspire men, or how to change his plans when things went wrong. He lacked *élan*. He lacked most of what one associates with the martial grandeurs of France.[6]

Reynaud became Prime Minister in March, 1940. He intended to rid himself of Gamelin. 'It would be criminal to leave this nerveless philosopher at the head of the French army,' he told Paul Baudouin, the Secretary of the War Cabi-

[6] Cf. Gamelin's book: *Servir: Les Armées Françaises de 1940*, the least interesting book on one of the most interesting moments in history.

net. Yet he could not unload Gamelin in time, for Gamelin was a protégé of Daladier, whom Reynaud had just ousted from the Premiership and whose support was needed if the new government were to survive. Reynaud was persistent. Had the Germans attacked three days later—on May 13 instead of on May 10—Gamelin would have been out, replaced probably by General Huntziger. This might have changed the Battle of France and the entire war, since it seems improbable that any general except Gamelin would have sent the best of the French armies and the only British army into northern Belgium and on to the Dutch frontier, where they were trapped and useless for the decisive days to come. They were trapped because Gamelin really believed that the Ardennes were impenetrable. And he could not imagine that he might be wrong. He had no alternative plans. One is reminded of the generals of Napoleon III.

Belgium's return to neutrality in 1936, after the reoccupation of the Rhineland, did not suggest new thoughts or new fears to this 'nerveless philosopher'. The Belgians would not meet with the French or the British to concoct a plan in case Belgium were invaded. The Belgians would not allow the French and British to move to the line of the River Dyle when the war began. Nevertheless, imperturbably, Gamelin kept all his eggs in one basket. He was self-convinced of three notions: that the Germans must invade through Belgium, and perhaps a bit of Holland; that the Belgian defence along the Albert canal, with the fortress of Eban Emael, would hold until the Allies arrived and took up their positions; and that the main battles would therefore take place along this line.

Side by side with his Dyle river day-dream Gamelin had the illusion that the war would last for years, giving the French ample time to replace any deficiencies, such as the lack of an air force. He also believed, before September 1939, that the war would never take place. He said that the moment war was declared Hitler and his régime would collapse. *Le jour où la guerre sera déclarée à l'Allemagne, Hitler s'effondera.*

The French were rash to have a commander-in-chief who (almost as adroit as Alice's White Queen) could believe three impossible things before breakfast: that there would be no war, that there would be no attack through the Ardennes, and that if war did come France would have lots of time.

Presumably the Germans knew Gamelin's plans. They obliged him by attacking Belgium and Holland with considerable force and great ferocity. Eban Emael fell on the second day (May 11). This ended all hope for a stand on the Albert canal, and all hope for Belgium in her hurtful neutrality unless other people took the trouble to beat the Germans.

When Gamelin heard of the explosion into Holland and Belgium, he gave orders for 'the Dyle plan' but added that it would be good to reach forward to Breda, in Holland. (The Dyle is a tiny river south of Antwerp and the plan involved an Allied line from Antwerp south to Dinant on the Meuse, and then reaching on northeast of Antwerp to Breda.) This meant that General Giraud's 7th Army (in reserve near Reims, an ideal spot for a counter-attack) should rush for the Dutch frontier, that Lord Gort's British Expeditionary Force should move toward Louvain,[7] and that General Blanchard's 1st Army (the best army in Europe, according to the Germans) should move vainly north of Namur, north of the Sambre, to meet an enemy whose only purpose was to delay him until it was too late to turn round and take part in the real battle which was to settle the Gallic phase of the war during the next few days.

Unlike Gamelin, the Germans were not planning a replay of 1914. Their attack to the north, ferocious and bloody as it became, was merely what Liddell Hart called 'the matador's cloak', the feint to fool Gamelin into putting his best troops into Flanders while the body blow came south through the Ardennes and across the Meuse into General Corap's unhappy

[7] Nine divisions advanced with the French on either flank. One division was on garrison duty in the Maginot Line Division of Field force trained for fighting.

9th Army: second-call reservists, and below strength, and lacking in equipment and spirit.

Once Guderian and Rommel with their Panzers (and with
the motorised infantry and artillery which could take over
when the tanks broke down) were all across the Meuse, there
was no hope for France. Her good troops and her Allies were
elsewhere. The reckless advance of German armour toward
Abbeville, and on to the sea, could only have been stopped by
an order from Hitler. Some German generals urged Hitler to

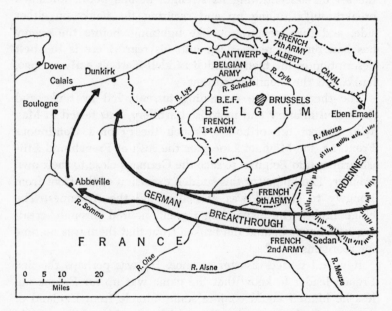

think twice about the dangers of this long, thin line from the
Meuse to the Channel, with great armies to the north and armies of a sort to the south. Manstein, however, had persuaded
Hitler that he, the genius-Fuehrer, had devised the whole astounding plan: the bottling up of the Allies in Flanders and
the sword's thrust through the heart of France to the sea. Once
Hitler thought an idea was his own, he knew it was inspired.

So Guderian and Rommel were allowed to show the world

what they had learned from two Englishmen: Sir Basil Liddell Hart and Major-General Fuller. Guderian had hired a translator to put all Liddell Hart's writings and speeches into German. General Fuller's books were published in Germany and his many articles in *The English Review* were attacked fiercely by the Old Guard in England.

One day in North Africa Rommel was complaining that some of his troops were slow to learn the methods of *blitzkrieg*. 'The division's command', he wrote, 'had not mastered the art of concentrating its strength at one point, forcing a breakthrough, rolling up and securing the flanks on either side, and then penetrating like lightning, before the enemy has had time to react, deep into his rear.' Here is the best description of the tactics which Liddell Hart, as early as 1920, had called 'the expanding torrent'.

The theory of 'the expanding torrent', led by tanks and motorised infantry and motorised artillery, was tested in May 1940 against the orthodox French theory of a Continuous Front, i.e. the Maginot Line plus the rush of French and British armies into Belgium to face the Germans close to their own frontier. The hinge for this sudden extension of the front from Longwy to Holland was at Sedan and the Ardennes. The hinge broke. The 'expanding torrent' poured through, creating such havoc behind the broken front that there was no time for reorganisation.[8]

Reynaud sensed disaster at once. He was perhaps the first French leader to know that the game was up for France unless he himself could conjure some miracle from England or America. Early on the morning of May 15, Churchill was told that Reynaud was on the telephone. 'He spoke in English', wrote Churchill, 'and evidently under stress. "We have been

[8] As all the world knows, the attempts at reorganisation were thwarted by wild columns of refugees with their prams and barrows. These were often sent on the road by false telephone orders to the local authorities. And they were always half-maddened, when not killed, by the howling Stukas. We shall see later that had England been invaded this particular form of hell-warfare would not have worked.

defeated." As I did not immediately reply he said again: "We have been defeated; we have lost the battle . . . The front is broken near Sedan; they are pouring through in great numbers with tanks and armoured cars." '

Churchill was reassuring. He was still thinking in terms of the First World War when offensives petered out after a few days, waiting for supplies. 'I did not comprehend', he wrote, 'the violence of the revolution effected since the last war by the incursion of a mass of fast-moving heavy armour.'

Reynaud comprehended, because Reynaud had been instructed by General de Gaulle. In 1934, the then Lieutenant-Colonel de Gaulle had published a small book: *Vers l'armée de métier*. This young officer knew that the rise of Hitler meant war and that the war would be won by disciples of the neglected English writers[9] and not by the disciples of Pétain and his 'continuous front'. De Gaulle urged that France should have, in addition to her conscripts, a small professional army manned by soldiers who had enlisted for six years: 'six divisions of the line and one light division, motorised throughout and armoured in part.' He also wanted 3,000 up-to-date tanks and 800 motorised machine-guns. He said this should be supported by a sufficient air force. He never defined 'sufficient' and it is doubtful if he foresaw (as the Germans did) the deadly effect of the airplane combined with motorised ground forces. Yet he had a vision of the shape of the war the Germans were planning. And he was a brave man for suggesting to his superior officers in France that they were silly.

Reynaud backed de Gaulle and they were both attacked by the 'best' authorities. This is why Churchill was misled when Reynaud told him the horrid truth so early on a May morning. The British advisers had been talking to Generals Gamelin

[9] They were not wholly neglected in France. André Beaufre, a young staff officer after the First World War and a general during the Second, thought Liddell Hart's doctrine 'as dazzling a discovery as the discovery of antiquity must have seemed to the men of the Renaissance after the conformist sterilities of medieval scholasticism'.

and Georges, who fed the British the same misinformation with which they blinded themselves. When these sleepy generals awoke to the fall of France, they blamed the troops—the brave, neglected troops—who when given a chance fought like the armies of Napoleon and when given no chance died in the slave-camps of Hitler. 'The French soldier,' wrote Gamelin, 'the citizen of yesterday, did not believe in the war . . . Today's call-up man did not receive the moral and patriotic education that would have prepared him for the drama in which the fate of his country was to be enacted.' And whose fault was that: the fault of the modest *boulanger* in Moulins? Or the modest *avocat* in Rennes? Or of our whole poisoned world ('chloroformed' said Clemenceau) which would not believe what Hitler had carefully told us?

The Moltke of the Franco-Prussian war said that 'one fault in the initial deployment of an army cannot be made good during the whole campaign'. The Dyle–Breda plan was the 'one fault'; but even this might have been repaired had there been time or room. Two Englishmen and one Frenchman (and doubtless many less articulate men) had noted during the thirties that the next war must move like lightning 'and must cease to be ere you can say "it lightens"'. After May 13–14, there was no time. And even worse, there was no room. From the Ardennes to the Channel is about 170 miles. From eastern Poland to the Caspian Sea, where one Russian army made its first effective stand, is some thousand miles. Such a retreat by the French would have taken them well out into the Atlantic, west of Ireland.

'After May 18,' writes Professor Chapman, 'the defeat of the Allies was not to be conjured, and the conversations of Reynaud with Churchill, with the two-minded French Cabinet, with an importunate de Gaulle and a Pétain over-persuaded of his capacities, with the deceived and outraged Weygand, are of less moment than the words of the chorus that accompany the slaying of Agamemnon.' Yet the fall was so terrible and so swift that nobody could bring himself to believe it—

unless Reynaud had truly grasped the whole horror when he telephoned to Churchill on May 15.

On May 18 Gamelin was sending a dozen of his best men to New York to contract for weapons which had not been built and which could not be built until new factories had arisen to mother them. On May 20 Weygand succeeded Gamelin and Pétain joined the Government as Vice-President of the Council. 'Marshal Pétain will remain at my side till victory is won,' said Reynaud on the radio. Never was a Prime Minister more deceived, for this vain old general was not only contemptuous of the Third Republic but he was eaten with ambition. He was soon to betray Weygand as a prelude to betraying France. And he hated the British for escaping, thus far, the horrors which had overcome his own country. On June 4 the Marshal told the American Ambassador in Paris, who in turn told President Roosevelt, what he thought of the British: they would fight to the last drop of French blood and then, with a good air force and a dominant fleet they would make a deal with Hitler, possibly accepting a government under a British fascist leader. This was the day when Churchill reported to Parliament on the results at Dunkirk, ending with his famous statement: 'We shall fight on the beaches, we shall fight on the landing grounds, we shall fight in the fields and in the streets, we shall fight in the hills; we shall never surrender.'

Edward Murrow asked Churchill to repeat this on the radio, for the benefit of America. When he had finished he covered the microphone with his hands and added, 'We'll hit them on the head with beer bottles, which is all we have to fight with.' The Marshal might have scorned such levity.

On May 21, some of the British who had survived their backward dash across Belgium tried to attack near Arras and cut the 'Panzer Corridor' which was here only twenty-five miles wide. The attack failed.

On May 23 Rommel wrote to his wife: 'Dearest Lu, . . . My division has been a blazing success. Dinant, Philipville, break-through the Maginot Line and advance in one night forty miles through France to Le Cateau, then Cambrai, Arras, always far in front of everybody else. Now the hunt is up against sixty encircled British, French and Belgian divisions. Don't worry about me. As I see it the war in France may be over in a fortnight'. Two days later he wrote: 'Dearest Lu . . . The division has lost up to date 27 officers killed and 33 wounded, and 1500 men dead and wounded. That's about 12 per cent casualties . . . The worst is now all over. There's little likelihood of any more hard fighting . . .'

The next day the retreat from Dunkirk began. On May 28 Belgium surrendered. France was now almost alone. Yet what else, in view of the French master-plan, could her Allies have done?

The French Commander-in-Chief devised and carried out the worthless 'Dyle–Breda Plan'—worthless largely because of Belgium's peace-time neutrality, but worthless nevertheless. Had the Allied armies been allowed into Belgium when the war began, had they held the line of the Dyle long before May 10 instead of leaping forward at the last moment and thus turning their backs on the main danger, the Ardennes invasion would have been suicidal even for Guderian and Rommel. With the Allies dug in along easily defensible positions behind Belgian rivers and canals, an equivalent of the Maginot Line would have been extended to Holland. The best British and French armoured divisions would have been free for a flank attack against an enemy venturing across the Meuse. Unhappily, because of Belgium's vain neutrality, these armoured troops were scrambling helter-skelter (or in some cases with faultless discipline) in the wrong direction.[10]

And the whole French army establishment (which did not include de Gaulle) was content to leave the Ardennes and

[10] Thinking—as even the great Churchill was still thinking—in terms of 1918, the French made sense. 'Crediting our enemies with our own procedure', said the Chief of Staff of General Georges, 'we had imagined that they would not attempt the passage of the Meuse until after they had brought up ample artillery: the five or six days necessary for that would have easily given us time to reinforce our own dispositions.'

Sedan, the hinge for the dash into Belgium, in the hands of third-rate troops. General Gamelin did not think that he might be mistaken and that the enemy might be fighting a new war and not the Schlieffen Plan again. One of his aides said on May 10: 'If you could have seen the General's face when I said the enemy were attacking Belgium in force, you would have known that he was right and that we would win the war.'

When Major-General Sir Edward Spears, on May 25, long after the game was up, asked Georges Mandel[11] 'What is the matter with the army?' he got a blunt answer: 'France could only fight with strong Allies. You, the English, certainly could not answer that description, and the United States do not exist so far as Europe is concerned . . . The French people felt they were not strong enough to face the Germans in the open field. And why, in any case, should they fight alone, they argued, for that is what it amounted to. No use talking to them in terms of sea power. War to them is a bloody business fought in the field, their own fields mostly.' This was not a sudden pessimism brought on by the German victories. Monsieur Berl reports that ever since 1934 Mandel had believed 'we can no longer save ourselves, all we can do is to be saved'.[12]

Mandel was right. How could the West have dreamed of being saved from Germany by France and a few British divisions? In 1914 Russia fought on France's side. 'The miracle of the Marne' gave Britain a breathing spell in which to train and equip large armies. And in time (long time) America joined the anti-German forces. In 1940 Russia was Germany's food-basket. Instead of Joffre's miracle of the Marne came Gamelin's horror of the Meuse, so the British could do nothing

---

[11] Ice-cold, fearless, incorruptible Mandel, who loved only Clemenceau and France, who had lost the first in 1929 and who knew without doubt, without hope, that he was losing the second in 1940. And with the death of France, he felt sure, went the death of Mandel. One of the proudest, strongest and most implacable Jews in Europe was not likely to survive the Third Reich.

[12] *Nous ne pouvons plus nous sauver, nous ne pouvons qu'être sauvés.*

for the moment except escape. Even when the old alliance was re-established—with Russia, Britain, a whole-hearted America and a diminished France side by side—Germany stood for years. With such an enemy on the doorstep, and all the world appeasing, *nous ne pouvons qu'être sauvés.*

Millions of dying men, had they remembered, should have cursed the American statesmen of 1919 who saw to it that France had neither the frontier on the Rhine nor the Anglo-American guarantee. Either might well have sufficed to prevent Hitler's war.

Nevertheless, in spite of the discouragement of the 'twenty-year armistice' contrived at Versailles, the French army might have striven harder to save itself and its country had some leader answered the question: 'Saved from what?' In *The Secret Conferences of Dr Goebbels* we learn that on May 30 the orders were: 'The most important task for the next few weeks will be to explain to the public . . . the need for a radical settling of accounts with France . . . the hatred of France is to be fanned afresh . . . The French must be pilloried as "niggerised sadists" . . . A state of affairs must be brought about, within a fortnight at the most, in which the entire German nation is consumed with anger and hatred against a France riddled with corruption and freemasonry.'

The French, however, were to hear a different tale. On June 14 Goebbels ordered: 'Two of the secret transmitters . . . are to describe with increasing benevolence how peace and order have come in the wake of the Germans.' The major theme in France was to be: 'Lay down your arms—it is all pointless.'

5

Dunkirk, in spite of its success as an evacuation, was another wedge to divide the French from the British. It was widely

rumoured that British troops were given preference over their
Allies. On May 29 Churchill ordered that one Frenchman
should be embarked for every Englishman. So far as possible
this was done. Yet in the end, when 338,226 men had been
saved, less than 13,000 of them were French. And 30,000
French troops, the last of the rearguard, had to be left behind.
This was correct procedure. The ratio between British and
French troops who were saved was correct in regard to the
number of soldiers from the two armies who were present at
the bridgehead. And Admiral Ramsay, before dawn on June 4,
when the official evacuation had ended, made a final effort to
lift the rearguard. He saved a few thousand. Dunkirk was now
under artillery fire. At 3.30 a.m. the last ships had to leave. The
French who stayed behind were part of the 1st Army, which
the Germans had judged the best in Europe. The discipline
and composure of these troops, sacrificed from the beginning
to Gamelin's misjudgment, impressed everyone who watched
their unhappy end.

Amid the confusion of impending defeat, the Germans could
spread the story that the British, having bled their Allies,
deserted as fast as possible. This did not encourage heroic last
stands. Yet there was such a last stand which has already become legendary and which finds its way into many of the
books dealing with these weeks. On the day Pétain asked for
an armistice the Wehrmacht reached the Loire at Saumur, the
site of the famous cavalry school. The cadets decided to resist
with their meagre weapons. They held the bridges for two
days, a *résistance héroique et désespérée*.

By the end of the 'miracle' of Dunkirk, the French had lost
the army of Belgium (twenty-two divisions), the army of
Holland (ten divisions), the British Expeditionary Force
(thirteen divisions), six out of seven of their own motorised
divisions, about 90,000 dead, plus 200,000 wounded, plus
1,900,000 prisoners and 'missing'. The Germans in what they
prematurely described as 'the greatest battle in world history',

had lost about 27,000 dead, 111,000 wounded and 18,300 missing.

On November 23, 1939, while urging his reluctant generals to attack westward as soon as the weather permitted, Hitler said it would cost him a million men to destroy France; but he added that it would cost the enemy as many men and that the enemy could not stand it.

6

Few remember the sequel to Dunkirk when the Royal Navy saved another 200,000 British and Allied troops from Cherbourg, St Malo and Brest. These were mostly the 'reconstituted B.E.F.': the 52nd Division, bits of the 1st Armoured Division, the 1st Canadian Division, etc. At St Valéry, on the night of June 10–11, the navy failed for the only time. Fog prevented the destroyers from entering the harbour. Most of the 51st (Highland) Division were taken prisoner.

'Audacious and imperturbable,' writes Peter Fleming, 'the Royal Navy stood out in the general ruin as the one force capable of frustrating the conqueror's designs.'

Meanwhile on land the irascible Weygand, who had been called home to preside over the humiliation of the army he had served all his life, told Reynaud that he could promise nothing. He would make a last stand behind the Somme and the Aisne; he would abandon the 'continuous front' which had obsessed and ruined Gamelin in favour of a 'hedgehog' system of defence in depth—each 'hedgehog' being ordered to hold out and harass from the rear after it had been bypassed.

Sensibly enough, Weygand expected to be defeated. His forces, as he said, were ridiculously weak. His air force scarcely existed. The British were recalcitrant about throwing away the last of their fighter planes. Still, said Weygand, the French army would do its best and when (not 'if') its best

proved insufficient the politicians must sue for peace. No nonsense about prolonging a lost war. Yet President Lebrun,
motoring south to catch up with his retreating Government,
wondered why there were so many soldiers on the roads since
Weygand insisted there were not enough on the Somme.

In fact, the French breakdown during the first decisive ten
days was not caused by lack of troops or of equipment, but by
their misuse. The Germans attacked with 136 divisions; the
Allies (including the Belgians and the Dutch) had 156. The
Germans had about 2,800 tanks, the Allies more than 4,000;[13]
but the French tanks were parcelled out in little groups among
the infantry, as in 1918. Only in the air were the Germans pre-
dominant.

By June 10 the French attempt to hold the Somme was
doomed. The Germans knew it, Hitler having proclaimed the
fall of France as early as June 5. Doubtless Weygand knew it,
since he had always been without hope. The public in France,
England and the United States did not know it. Even the most
experienced correspondents could not grasp that France had
fallen in a few weeks. And the air was full of lies. Alistair
Horne quotes Radio Strasbourg on June 12: 'While the German army suffers unheard-of losses, the French army remains
intact.' Judging by their efforts to keep France in the war, one
wonders whether the Prime Minister and the Cabinet in Great
Britain knew that the end had come.

7

By Friday, June 14, when the Germans entered Paris, the
French Government was settled into its brief chaos at Bordeaux. Reynaud had sent de Gaulle to London to see what
the British could find in the way of transport for troops and

[13] Rommel's Panzer division, which made such havoc, had 218 tanks,
half of them Czech-built.

munitions to North Africa. What troops, since the French army was breaking up? And what munitions, since nobody had any? Or if the French still had abundant arms, as asserted at Riom, nobody knew where they were.[14]

In any case, when the Government finally straggled into Bordeaux the town became an inferno of plots and confusion. 'This dreary, rotten, collapsing world of Bordeaux,' wrote Major-General Sir Edward Spears who had to watch the pitiful last act as special representative from the Prime Minister. Some, like Reynaud and Mandel, wanted to go on fighting though they couldn't decide where; Weygand and most of his generals wanted to stop the slaughter; and Pétain, encouraged by Laval, wanted to subject France to his own form of fascism. Laval's motives were simple: he hated England and admired Hitler. He thought he was doing France a favour by subjecting her to 'the wave of the future', the 1,000-year Reich which he hoped might be grateful to Laval. Pétain's motives were more complicated and less reputable. He had long been the hero of every right-wing enemy of the Third Republic. In 1936 the *Croix de Feu*[15] published a pamphlet, *C'est Pétain qu'il nous faut*, which outlined the semi-religious fascism which was to flourish at Vichy. The Marshal believed that France had sinned, had worshipped false gods, and must be punished. The punishment he had in mind was to be ruled by Pétain.

[14] The question whether France had vast unused resources which were wasted by inefficiency cannot be answered on the present evidence. Major-General Sir Edward Spears seems confident that the answer is 'Yes'; but he relies largely on the Riom trials held under the Vichy Government in 1942. The purpose of the trials was to blame everybody who was absent. Daladier was copious with facts or fancies: 'the Germans found 750 anti-tank guns in the depots, and over 2,000 tractors unused . . . At St Denis there was enough to equip 30–35 divisions. Why were they not equipped? . . . Why did the tanks remain in the back areas?' The Public Prosecutor gently reminded, 'You were the Minister for War.' 'Yes,' said Daladier, 'but I was not a store-keeper.' The answer seems inadequate.

[15] Fascist.

On March 30, 1940, he said to the Minister of Works (Menzie), 'They'll need me by the second half of May' ('*Ils aurent besoin de moi dans la seconde quinzaine de mai*'). Pride and ambition, politics and religiosity, with Lucifer in the form of Laval egging him on; no wonder the Germans, hoping to save themselves trouble, threw Pétain a slice of France upon which to practise his creed.

Yet Pétain had reason to despise the democracy of the Third Republic. On May 19, 1917, he had been made Commander-in-Chief. Three days later came the mutinies in the French army. Perhaps only Pétain could have coped with them, for the troops rightly believed that Pétain wanted no more offensives and was content to wait as quietly as possible for the Americans. On May 29 Pétain reported on the mutinies to the Minister of War. The report is a great State Document: cold, exact, ruthless and politically fearless. It ends with what Correlli Barnett describes as a 'beautifully organised and absolutely devastating indictment of French politics and French society in the third spring of the war'. Pétain attacks the press, the politicians (especially those who visited the front) and the whole tone of life in the capital city. He was right in 1917 and he had not changed his mind by 1940.

Bordeaux in June of 1940 was confused and embittered by attempts, among the bravest of the French, to pretend that the defeat which had taken place could somehow be avoided. The British applauded anyone who insisted against all hope that there must be a place where the French could go on fighting. A Franco-British Agreement of March, 1940, had promised that neither country would make peace without the consent of the other. Weygand's opinion was that the Agreement should not be honoured. When an army is beaten in the field, he said, there is nothing to do except admit the truth and stop fighting. One can see why Churchill took a different view and why the British encouraged every wild French plan for escaping from the facts.

First, there was the dream of the Breton Redoubt, into which

the remaining French divisions could withdraw and where
they could be joined by the British when the fugitives from
Dunkirk had been rearmed. Who would provide the air cover
without which Brittany, dense with troops, would become an
abattoir? Not the French, who said their air force was consumed. And not, presumably, the British, whose remaining
fighters could beat the Luftwaffe over the fields of England
but not over the more distant fields of Brittany.

Then there was the myth of North Africa and the rallying
of the French Empire. Weygand described the Empire as 'a
pack of blacks over whom you will have no control from the
moment you're beaten'—not a bad prophecy in the light of
history. And assuming that half a million French troops could
reach North Africa, who would feed them? Who would arm
them? Not Britain or the United States, both of whom were
without arms. The United States, amid outcries from the
peacemongers, were sending First World War rifles to the
denuded British.

Yet on June 16 there came a flicker of life. De Gaulle in
London telephoned Reynaud in Bordeaux and read him the
British offer of an indissoluble union between the French and
British peoples, all citizens of both countries becoming members of the new union. This extraordinary offer was almost
à l'échelle de l'époque.[16] Reynaud was reanimated. 'Does he
really mean this?' he asked de Gaulle, referring to Churchill.
Then Churchill himself took the receiver and told Reynaud
it was a decision of the whole British Cabinet.

Reynaud's joy was quickly squashed. Bordeaux had become
a cesspool for the defeated, for the men with cold hearts.
These unwise men said the offer was a scheme to get Germans
to go on killing Frenchmen while the British prepared their
defences behind the Channel. Others said they did not want
France to become a Dominion. Pétain agreed with anyone
who had no hope.

[16] Jean Monnet and Vansittart had first dreamed of this plan.

The curt rejection of Britain's offer broke Reynaud. He resigned, expecting to be asked to form a new Government deprived of cowards. The President called on Pétain, who produced his list of ministers and formed his new Government overnight with suspicious speed. His first act was to ask the Spanish Ambassador to approach the Germans for an armistice.

8

A cease-fire is what the old man should have requested. After a cease-fire the Dutch set up a Government-in-Exile in Britain. Throughout the war they served the anti-German cause with whatever they could extract from their homeland and their Empire. So did other countries whose governments were powerless to prevent defeat but not powerless to prevent dishonour. This was a problem which did not trouble Pétain, who was zealous for defeat since defeat meant the imposition of his own New Order on whatever bits and pieces of France the Germans left him.

Pétain, infirm in spirit, did not represent his country; but a woman did, a woman passionate for France: Eve Curie. She, too, struggled in the miasma at Bordeaux, watching the rise of Laval and Pétain. One day she broke down before Major-General Sir Edward Spears: 'Don't you see it, they are all double-crossing you . . . These poltroons will say that they will reject anything but reasonable terms, but they know that once they have begun to negotiate they will have to do the Germans' bidding . . . You are being fooled, fooled! . . . They must not dishonour France. That is the only thing that would really kill France. France can survive if she is not dishonoured.'[17]

[17] I saw a lot of Eve Curie during the subsequent months in New York. With her flaming intensity she seemed to embody what I thought, and think, to be the spirit of France.

Misprising England and pleased with himself, confident that France must expiate her sinfulness through suffering, Pétain chose Germany and spurned the offer of Union which might have renewed Europe. The French armies (and the Belgian and the Dutch and the British) had been beaten in the field. The Union could not repair that disaster. Neither the Breton Redoubt nor the flight to North Africa would have become feasible because of Union; yet rich new hopes and energies might have been let loose. Here was a plan for a better Europe equivalent in daring to that of the barbarians. Spengler had taught Hitler that the wars of parochial nationalism must lead to a new age of Caesars. Luckily the Spengler-Caesar was half-mad. Yet he nearly killed us all, and because of him the world today is in widespread disorder.

What might have happened had the great offer been accepted? In the first place, there would have been no Pétain to tell all Frenchmen to cower and to obey. People in uniform tend to obey the highest rank in the land; so Pétain's orders put to sleep an army of Frenchmen who might have joined de Gaulle, fled to the Colonies, or started the guerrilla warfare which Churchill urged upon them and which in the end they fought with ferocity. Why not in the beginning? Chiefly because the arch-defeatist, and the new head of state, was a Marshal of France.

Naturally, this peace-demanding Marshal was vexed at the thought of England continuing after France had failed. As early as June 12 he told Major-General Sir Edward Spears that since France could not continue the struggle England should seek peace for she could not carry on alone. 'You have no army,' he said. 'What could you achieve where the French army has failed?' He added that it was 'cruel self-deception' to think that we [the English] could stand up to the Germans alone for more than a month.

The next day Churchill told Reynaud: 'The war will continue, and can but end in our destruction or our victory.' Thus the Marshal, and thus the Prime Minister.

9

Meanwhile in the United States there came the first, faint sign
that anybody, except the President and some foreign correspondents, saw the danger which faced the country. Reynaud
on June 14 had appealed to President Roosevelt dramatically:
'Unless you can give France to understand, in the hours ahead,
that the United States will enter the war in the very near
future, the destiny of the world will change.' A natural plea,
but without reality. This was the President whose Congress
had refused him the power to embargo arms against an aggressor unless the victim were refused arms at the same time;
the President who was not even allowed to join his country to
the World Court.

Most Americans, in that June of 1940, believed three huge
lies: first, that the United States had been dragged into the
Kaiser-war by a sinister combination of British propaganda
and Wall Street; second, that Germany had a legitimate grievance against France and that, therefore, no one should take
too seriously the deadly promises of *Mein Kampf;* third, that
in spite of America's insufficient navy the Atlantic and Pacific
Oceans were a protection against Europe and Asia, instead
of being a broad highway for invaders.

Nourished on such nonsense, the people of the United
States were largely isolationist, especially if they lived some
1,500 miles inland from either ocean. The President, luckily,
knew the meaning of sea-power. He sensed the danger to his
country as France fell and Britain was threatened; but he
could not proclaim the truth without losing his public and
his authority in Congress. He needed a non-partisan group
of citizens to say much more than he could dare endorse and
to ask for much more than he could hope to accomplish. Then

he might move gingerly in the direction of saving his sleeping country.

The nucleus of such a group appeared on June 10, the day that Mussolini declared war on France and that the 'one last battle' of the Somme was lost. In the morning papers, from coast to coast, appeared 'A Summons to Speak Out' signed by thirty American citizens. 'The frontier of our national interest is now on the Somme', said the thirty; '[our] resources cannot be made available fast enough to hold the German army in check on the European continent or to prepare for the eventual attack on American interests so long as the United States remains legally neutral . . . The United States should immediately give official recognition to the fact and to the logic of the situation—by declaring that a state of war exists between this country and Germany . . . The undersigned, as individuals, invite those citizens of the United States who share these views to express them publicly.'

Among 'the undersigned' were a Bishop, a retired Admiral who had lately been Chief of Naval Operations, several newspaper editors, authors, economists and business men. They were well scattered about the country, so this could not be dismissed as a regional document or as the work of New York Jews.

The summons got adequate newspaper coverage but fewer front pages than we had hoped, because of Mussolini's inconvenient Declaration on the same day. Nevertheless, the unspeakable had been spoken. People who shared our views now knew where to find their friends and combine their influences. All this came much too late to be of the slightest use to France, or to arouse interest in England, where deeds, not words, were needed. We did not know, we could not know in view of the stunned world's refusal to accept the facts, that France had lost her battle on the very day we talked about a frontier on the Somme. Yet the fact that only thirty American war-mongers could be mobilised on June 10, 1940, shows how misplaced were the last hopes of the unhappy Reynaud.

So, as I said in my Preface, from June 22, 1940, when the French petitioned for an armistice, until June 22, 1941, when Hitler invaded Russia, there was only Britain to save the West. Laval and Hitler were confident that Britain would collapse at once. King George VI disagreed. He wrote to his mother: 'Personally I feel happier now that we have no allies to be polite to and to pamper.'

And a Scottish Lowland farmer said to Sir John Balfour, 'Ah weel, I suppose we'll just be more compact noo.'

III
Britain: September 3
to June 22

1

The Chiefs of Staff, for reasons which they could not define, shared King George's pleasure at being left alone. General Ismay[1] in his *Memoirs* writes: 'So far from being alarmed, we were relieved, nay, exhilarated. Henceforward everything would be simpler. We were masters of our own fate.' Just before Dunkirk, Ismay recalls, Churchill asked the Chiefs of Staff whether Britain could continue the war if France fell. The reply 'was a curious document. The first twelve paragraphs were devoted to showing that the enemy had the whip hand in almost every sphere.' The conclusion was: Yes, we believe we can win. 'The report contented Churchill,' says Ismay. It would certainly have contented the British people, though heaven knows why.

Even the melancholy Leonard Woolf wrote, after the final severance from France, 'It was then, however, that we like so many other people had that strange sense of relief—almost of exhilaration—at being left alone, "shut of" all encumbrances, including our allies—"now we can go it alone", in our muddled, makeshift, empirical English way.'

[1] At that time Major-General Sir Hastings Ismay, Chief of Staff to the Minister of Defence (Winston Churchill); later Lord Ismay.

Ever since the days of appeasement the British had assumed that if Germany conquered bases in the Low Countries the attack from the air would be crushing. The Germans now held the coastline from the North Cape to the Pyrenees. So why the uncanny optimism which did not arise until France proclaimed her total defeat? Leonard Woolf describes a far less happy feeling early in June while France was still fighting. He and Virginia Woolf and Rose Macaulay and Kingsley Martin talked mournfully until 2 a.m.: 'Kingsley, diffusing his soft charcoal gloom, prophesied the defeat of France and the invasion of Britain within five weeks. A Fifth Column would get to work; the Government would move off to Canada leaving us to a German Pro-Consul, a concentration camp, or suicide. We discussed suicide while the electric light gradually faded and finally left us sitting in complete darkness.'

How seriously did they take their talk of suicide? Among my friends, Rebecca West, Leonard Woolf and his wife, Harold Nicolson and his wife, and Rose Macaulay perhaps, were equipped for death. Kingsley Martin carried morphia but did not think he would use it in spite of his 'soft charcoal gloom'. I always felt that the pills and the talk were chiefly an expression of contempt for the idea of living under Germans. I doubt whether any of them believed in their bones that Germans were the sort of people who could win the war, let alone run the world. It was partly a matter of prose style: a heavy-footed boastfulness versus an Alice-in-Wonderland touch. While the Luftwaffe was destroying Poland, the British Foreign Secretary told the Italian Ambassador that Goering was 'a mixture of the Duke of Devonshire, his head gamekeeper and Al Capone, all topped off with a schoolboy'. Remember Churchill and his beer bottles.

And remember 'Bolo House': in 1918 the new Air Board was housed in the Hotel Cecil in London. The young men who were flying in France disapproved of the Board for lack of boldness. So they named the Cecil 'Bolo House' after a French spy who had been shot. Everyone in Bolo House, they said, was 'either actively interfering with the progress of the war or doing nothing to help'. Such a zany approach to authority is stronger than Teutonic respectfulness.

Prose style may seem a strange ally in a world war; but it is not. Consider Churchill's genius in turning 'Local Defence Volunteers' into 'Home Guard' and 'Communal Feeding Centres' into 'British Restaurants'. In both cases the first name might have been invented by a Gauleiter; the second is English and rings with hope.

Albert Sorel wrote of the British: 'Their history is full of these alternations between an indifference that seems to stem from decadence and a fury that disconcerts their enemies.' From the day France fell the British were in a state of quiet fury which was often to disconcert the Germans. After one so-called peace offer from the Nazis, Churchill wondered why Hitler could not understand that the British 'now meant to have his blood or perish in the attempt'. One can see why the Fuehrer was confused. Only yesterday Ribbentrop was telling him the English would never fight.

The British also felt, after the fall of France, that Pétain and his entourage did not represent the opinions of wise men anywhere. This was not 'just another war', as Weygand and Pétain seemed to think, a war which could end in an honourable defeat and an honourable peace: not William I of Germany but Genghis Khan as Reynaud had insisted. Odd as it may sound today, the war presented a clear choice between good and evil, or between much-better and much-worse. The seemingly inane optimism of the British in June, 1940, sprang from a half-belief that some day even foreigners must see that their own lives were at stake—or their own civilisation, to use a wornout word. Included in these lives (or this civilisation) was everybody's public library and picture gallery, and everybody's private soul. When this truth finally became clear, friends might begin to rally round.

Many Frenchmen saw the truth from the beginning, saw that Britain must survive because if she didn't there was nothing left. Roger Martin du Gard wrote: *'Toute espérance passe par la victoire anglaise . . . Comme il n'y a pas d'autre espérance, il ne peut y avoir d'autre foi.'* He added sadly, *'Mais la plupart ne croyaient rien de tout.'* Nevertheless, many Frenchmen who still had hope found their way to England by devious routes, reassuring the islanders that stubbornness was correct.

Not that they needed reassurance, for they knew it was their strange task to stand alone and see what happened. Neither England nor France could have a future unless somebody beat the Nazis. Toward the end of June, 1940, there was only one candidate for that job.

Another would-be candidate arrived toward the middle of the month: General de Gaulle, with no money and few followers. As Claud Cockburn wrote: 'The people who never can see how to make more than four out of two times two . . . had a jolt. France, like Evadne in *The Maid's Tragedy*, had brought many people near to

> *. . . that dull calamity*
> *To that strange misbelief in all the world,*
> *And all things that are in it.*

General de Gaulle . . . [was] an escape from dull calamity . . . The highlights of life and history are produced by the occasions and personalities which make two times two equal seven. This is a function of *mystique.'*

Miracles and fairy stories were in short supply at that time in London. Those of us who loved France and were not in high positions were never subjected to the haughtiness or the sardonic jokes or the vindictiveness of de Gaulle. We wove our fairy tale with pleasure and in innocence. We were lucky to admire and not to know enough to doubt. Claud Cockburn comments: 'He [de Gaulle] could never resist a joke even when to play it was obviously against his best interests. Most of his jokes were about as harmless as a hand grenade after the pin has been taken out.' Neither Churchill nor Roosevelt enjoyed the jokes and they hated the haughtiness and they deplored the vindictiveness. The rest of us savoured our miracle: the impossible man at the impossible time doing what could not be done.

Free people who have influence on their governments must go to all their wars too late and too little. They listen to leaders who tell them not to worry, that the devil is an honourable man. Duff Cooper laments this when he mourns the great cause for which England might have fought at the time of Munich, and adds: 'We were fighting now neither for a principle nor for others. We were fighting for our lives.' Yet there is another side to the story, as Duff Cooper himself points out in an earlier book when he quotes from a letter signed by a dozen 'rank and file members of the Trade Union Movement'. It was a plea for conscription. 'Is it not time the working man began to think' (says the letter). 'It is he who will take the can back if war comes. It is he who will be fighting in the trenches while the bombers smash in his little home . . . Our homes, the progress of our class, the peace and freedom of this country and of the world, demands that this country be put under orders now—orders to wealth as well as labour, orders to the country as a whole.'

This was before the war started, but after Hitler had made a joke of his promises by destroying Czechoslovakia. Would Trade Unionists have been demanding conscription had Britain gone to war, chivalrously, in the autumn of 1938? Or was it necessary to make one more effort at supping with the devil so that the whole country might see that there was no recourse but force? The unity of the British people in a seemingly hopeless spot has been one of the marvels of modern times. May it have come in part from the patience verging on humility which was displayed by 'the men of Munich'? Or was it simply an ancient pride?

According to a Gallup Poll taken when France fell, only three per cent of these astonishing people thought they might lose the war. They were unaccustomed to being invaded; they always expected miracles from their navy; the air, a new terror, was too unknown, too unpredictable, to destroy public confidence.

2

One officer in high command agreed wholeheartedly with the King's happiness at being left without allies: Air Chief Marshal Sir Hugh (later Lord) Dowding. He was the Chief of Fighter Command.

When the war began, the Government wanted Dowding to broadcast a reassurance to the nation. He asked how many fighter squadrons he would have when the Luftwaffe attacked.[2] He was told fifty-two, so he made the broadcast. He did not say that the bombers would never get through, unlike Goering who made just such a promise to the Germans.[3] Yet Dowding did suggest that the Luftwaffe would not ruin his Fighter Command and therefore would not control the skies over the Channel for an invasion of England. The brief war in France, however, consumed almost half his precious squadrons, not only to support the British Expeditionary Force but to support the French as well.

On May 13 General Gort told the Secretary of State for War (Anthony Eden): 'We have to support in the air not only the B.E.F. but also our Allies . . . Our main defence in the air is fighters . . . I earnestly hope the War Cabinet will decide to give additional assistance.' Churchill writes of these sad days: 'The burden of General Gamelin's, and indeed of all the French

[2] Twelve planes in the air per squadron, with four in reserve on the ground.

[3] Before the war began Goering announced: 'If an enemy bomber ever succeeds in reaching the Ruhr my name is not Hermann Goering. You can call me Meier.' Peter Townsend comments: 'Only nine months later the whole of Germany would be doing so.'

High Command's remarks, was insistence on their inferiority in the air and earnest entreaties for more Squadrons of the Royal Air Force, bomber as well as fighter, but chiefly the latter.' Gamelin even asked for British fighters to attack German tanks; but Churchill told him that was a job for the artillery.

The pressure on the British to become foolhardy and over-generous with planes was almost irresistible. Their land forces were inadequate. The French did not understand the use of navies. 'No use talking to them in terms of sea-power,' as Mandel had told General Spears. 'War to them is a bloody business fought in the field, their own fields mostly.' Now their French fields were stained with blood. And the British had first-class fighter planes. Why not fling them all into the battle? The answer is that France today might well be a slave of a real 1,000-year Reich, had Churchill given all that was asked of him. And he nearly did.

Between May 10 and the fall of France, the R.A.F. lost 959 planes of which 477 were fighters. Dowding's friend and biographer, Robert Wright, says that after the worst had happened on the Continent Dowding told Lord Halifax (the Foreign Secretary), 'Thank God we're now alone.'

Mr Wright also quotes the Air Chief Marshal on 'the atmosphere of devastating strain when I was fighting the Germans and the French and the Cabinet and the Air Ministry and now and again the navy for good measure . . . I was already down to thirty-six squadrons against the fifty-two I was supposed to have.' And each time the Prime Minister flew the Channel for a disconsolate meeting he gave the French a few more squadrons. Who could blame him? He loved the French and they were his Allies, and his own country in the midst of the disaster had been able to contribute little.

And who could blame Dowding for resisting fiercely? His Fighter Command, he had been told from on high, was a defensive weapon to save England (and thus the world) from capitulation. 'Mine was purely the role of trying to stop the possibility of an invasion,' he said. Yet his planes were being frittered away for no better reason than that the French air force was woeful and incompetent.[4]

Had Fighter Command been designed to support a great army on the Continent it should have had more than twice its strength. This would have been a political decision, and the politicians did not so decide. Dowding was left with his Home Defence Force, which was all that had been ordered, and he had to watch it being consumed in support of a British retreat and evacuation (which was correct), and then in support of a vain French stand on the Somme (which was incorrect).

By the middle of May, Fighter Command was only half as strong as Dowding had been promised. No wonder he was glad when France fell and the drain stopped. No wonder he said to an astonished British general, before Dunkirk, that the best thing the B.E.F. could do was to lay down its arms and run. 'You are doing no good in France,' he implied, 'and the more you prolong your defeat the less chance we shall have of saving England.'

After Gort's appeal on May 13, thirty-two more fighters were sent to France. Dowding asked to appear before the Cabinet. He felt that even at the cost of his job he must explain what would happen to England if his command were left to bleed to death. On May 15 (the day that Reynaud telephoned to the Prime Minister that France had lost her battle) Dowding met the War Cabinet. He had prepared a graph of what was happening. He put it before Winston Churchill, saying: 'If the present rate of wastage continues for another fortnight, we shall not have a single Hurricane left in France *or in this country*.'[5]

The Military Assistant Secretary (General Sir Ian Jacob)

---

[4] The British refusal of planes helps us to understand the French refusal of Union. The first was wise. The second may have been a disaster. We shall never know.

[5] Italics Dowding's, verbally.

wrote later: 'The decision was one of the hardest to make in the whole of the war, and opinion swayed back and forth. Dowding, an austere man, spoke up clearly and well, and his case for retaining the whole of Fighter Command for home defence was very strong. The Prime Minister was torn in two.' Churchill was indignant at being defeated by the facts. In his romantic and endearing way, he thought that the men who served him could always produce a miracle if he insisted.

Miracles were no longer on tap for those who lacked air power. Churchill accepted Dowding's distasteful truths. The Cabinet said, 'No more planes to France.'

Within an hour, in the garden at No. 10 Downing Street, the Prime Minister changed his mind and sent four more fighter squadrons to France. This is heart-warming (though it was not so to Dowding) and thoroughly Churchillian. He would always give all to France, for the honour of his beloved England, except the last plane needed to save England. And since he believed in miracles, and was a minor miracle himself, he gambled with those four squadrons and with a few more later. His gamble came off, but only by the skin of his teeth.

Churchill wrote, in his history of the Second World War: 'The hard question of how much we could send from Britain without leaving ourselves defenceless and thus losing the power to continue the war pressed itself henceforward upon us. Our own natural promptings and many weighty military arguments lent force to the incessant, vehement French appeals. On the other hand, there was a limit, and that limit if transgressed would cost us our life.'

On the evening after talking to the War Cabinet, Dowding wrote a letter, saying that the 'limit' had already been reached, if not transgressed. This may be the most important document of the lonely year. Addressed to the Under-Secretary of State at the Air Ministry (who would have to show it to the Prime Minister), the letter assumed that defeat on the Continent was a possibility.[6]

[6] Unknown even to the British High Command, defeat was already a certainty.

'In this case', wrote Dowding, 'I presume that there is no-one who will deny that England should fight on . . . for this purpose it is necessary to retain some minimum fighter strength in this country and I must request that the Air Council will inform me what they consider this minimum strength to be, in order that I may make my dispositions accordingly.

'I would remind the Air Council that the last estimate which they made as to the force necessary to defend this country was 52 Squadrons and my strength has now been reduced to the equivalent of 36 Squadrons.

'Once a decision has been reached as to the limit on which the Air Council and the Cabinet are prepared to stake the existence of the country, it should be made clear to the Allied Commanders on the Continent that not a single aeroplane from Fighter Command beyond the limit will be sent across the Channel, no matter how desperate the situation may become . . .

'I believe that, if an adequate fighter force is kept in this country, if the fleet remains in being . . . we should be able to carry on the war single handed for some time, if not indefinitely. But, if the Home Defence Force is drained away in desperate attempts to remedy the situation in France, defeat in France will involve the final, complete and irremediable defeat of this country.'[7]

At this vital moment, when Britain was truly at stake, Dowding was amused to remember his disappointment when the promise to make him Chief of Air Staff was broken. How lucky, he now thought. As C.A.S. he would have been battling prematurely with Churchill to save Fighter Command. He would have been saying what *would happen* and not what *was happening*. 'A few days earlier', as Peter Townsend puts it, 'and he would have been unable to convince the Prime Minister of the seriousness of the position; a few days later and the damage would have been irrevocable.' Broken promises are seldom so fruitful.

[7] This letter has been framed and now hangs in a place of honour in the Royal Air Force College at Cranwell.

Churchill was in Paris when Dowding's letter was received. While the Chief of Air Staff was begging the Cabinet to take heed of the Air Chief Marshal's sombre warning, word came from France that Churchill wanted permission to send six more fighter squadrons to his ally. Half-heartedly and half-bitterly, the Cabinet agreed that the six squadrons might be allowed to operate over France, and to refuel in France, while returning to their bases in southern England at the end of each mission.

The strain of these decisions to refuse the French is pictured by Ismay who went with Churchill on each visit to France. On June 11, when the game was up and the 'offensive' on the Somme had failed, Weygand lectured Churchill at Briare. A cardinal principle of strategy was to concentrate all available forces at the decisive point. 'Here', said Weygand, 'is the decisive point. Now is the decisive moment. The British ought not to keep a single fighter in England. They should all be sent to France.' Ismay was scared lest Churchill—'generous, warm-hearted, courageous and with a pronounced streak of optimism'—might give way. After a long pause the Prime Minister spoke slowly: 'This is not the decisive point. This is not the decisive moment. The decisive moment will come when Hitler hurls his Luftwaffe against Britain. If we can keep command of the air over our own island—that is all I ask —we will win it all back for you.' Then to soften the blow he added: 'Of course, if it is best for France in her agony that her army should capitulate, let there be no hesitation on our account. Whatever happens here, we are resolved to fight on and on for ever and ever and ever.'

Reynaud asked what England could do against the whole might of Germany. Churchill reverted to his beer bottles. He said the British would drown as many Germans as possible on the way over and *frapper sur le tête* those who got ashore. The irascible Weygand may not have been amused.

Thus at last the final, final-decision was taken: 'No more squadrons of fighters will leave the country whatever the needs

of France.' At the last minute of the last hour, Dowding had
his way. His contemporary and fellow Wykehamist, General
Wavell, warned him that his days were numbered: Churchill
had asked for a miracle and all he got was dire mathematics.
Yet Dowding was left in office long enough to win the Battle
of Britain.[8]

3

The French called it the *drôle de guerre*, the Americans 'the
phoney war'; but Chamberlain and Churchill spoke of 'the
twilight war', so I shall use that phrase. The seemingly senseless
months of delay were not so frustrating to the British as to
the French, because the British navy and merchant marine
were active and in constant danger. Yet the twilight war was
hard on morale.

Thus on October 6, 1939, the Minister of Transport[9] noted:
'The great difficulty at the moment seems to be the precise
definition of our war aims, and there is little doubt that there
is in the country a very great sense of bewilderment. Every
Minister . . . has been impressed with the doubts and in many
cases apathy, expressed in conversation the last few weeks
and by no means least in the House of Commons itself.'

After the fall of Poland, as Harold Macmillan admits in his
Memoirs, there was 'a smell of peace in the air'. Lloyd George
in the House of Commons (playing the part of Pétain as

[8] Years later Churchill wrote: 'Air Chief Marshal Dowding . . . had
declared to me that with twenty-five squadrons of fighters he could
defend the Island against the whole might of the German Air Force.'
Dowding commented: 'How Mr Churchill . . . ever came to put such
an absurd statement into my mouth I simply do not know. I had just
been waging a desperate battle in the Cabinet to retain the equivalent of
thirty-six squadrons against the fifty-two squadrons which was the Air
Staff estimate of my requirements.'

[9] Captain the Rt Hon. Euan Wallace.

Churchill later charged) raised his mellow and once all-persuasive voice in favour of stopping the war and calling a conference to discuss 'any proposals for peace which are specific, detailed and broad'. Duff Cooper attacked him for disgracing his country. A Welsh Labour member was equally virulent; so Goebbels got small profit from what might have been a bonanza: an author of the Treaty of Versailles obsequious before Hitler.

Bernard Shaw was more useful to the little Nazi wizard of the air-waves. In a letter to the *New Statesman and Nation* Shaw demanded to know what he was fighting for. 'Mr Chamberlain has cleared up that question to a certain point,' he admitted. 'He declares that we are not out for territorial conquest or material acquisitions of any sort. This means that the war is a purely ideological one. That is, we shall not cease from military fight, nor shall our swords sleep in our hand, until we have forcibly smashed National Socialism in Germany and Communism in Russia, and replaced both by the British Constitution.'

Maynard Keynes, repenting at last of his 'different hope' about the Germans, wrote to the same paper: 'The intelligentsia of the Left were loudest in demanding that Nazi aggression should be resisted at all costs. When it comes to a showdown, scarce four weeks have passed before they remember they are pacifists and write defeatist letters to your column, leaving the defence of freedom to Colonel Blimp and the Old School Tie, for whom Three Cheers.'

Meanwhile Chamberlain, with an optimism reminiscent of Gamelin, was beginning to think that the war would end itself. 'I have a "hunch"', he wrote on November 5, 'that the war will be over before the spring. It won't be by defeat in the field but by German realization that they *can't* win and it isn't worth their while to go on getting thinner and poorer when they might have instant relief and perhaps not have to give up anything they really care about.'

Such desultory chatter and vague hopefulness are bound to

arise when there is a war with no land-fighting, when the chief
reminder of war is boredom. The discussion of war aims (or
of a sudden, miraculous peace) becomes a form of vice since
it is meaningless and effects nothing and holds out false hopes.
When Churchill became Prime Minister, and the real war ex-
ploded, he set himself against all such gossip, insisting that
there was only one aim: Victory.[10] The politically luckless
Harold Nicolson incurred the P.M.'s grave reproof (and it
could be most grave) by writing an article for an American
paper on war aims. This was picked up by the British press
and was seen at No. 10 Downing Street.

Churchill was right. War aims, aside from victory, are bound
to be rose-tinted and to suggest that the world will become a
pleasanter place later. Why should it? Does a man become
gentler, wiser, more imaginative, because he has thrown
some assassins out of his house with whatever requisite violence? The purpose of the great wars of my lifetime has been
to clear the house of Germans. This has been done; but should
we thus grow kinder to children or more generous to old-age
pensioners?

Our two world wars have killed many of the best men in a
dozen countries. Between us all, we have starved and tortured and massacred countless millions; but Germans do not
now control France or Britain or Russia or the United States,
or for that matter the world. This was the yes-or-no question
posed by the wars. And the answer, for the Germans, was 'no'.

The price was high: the disintegration of Europe, the creation of a new and fearsome balance of power, the transforma-
tion of all Empires and of most nations. And life is still unjust.
Hence the repeated complaint, especially from the young,
that we win the wars but nothing golden happens. Again, why
should it? We did not fight to make the world kinder, or to
make it safe for democracy. How could we, since democracy
is by nature insecure? We fought for our lives. Anyone who

[10] During the twilight war, on land, both victory and defeat seemed
impossible.

we should have refrained might read *Mein Kampf* and
᠁r.

᠁ᴜᴄ the war had notable effects upon the English people,
effects which were in no sense war-aims but rather war-results.
When the blitz was raging, J. B. Priestley described one of
these effects: 'It so happens that this war, whether those at
present in authority like it or not, has to be fought as a citizen's
war. There is no way out of that because in order to defend
and protect this island, not only against possible invasion but
also against all the disasters of aerial bombardment, it has
been found necessary to bring into existence a new network
of voluntary associations such as the Home Guard, the Ob-
server Corps, all the A.R.P. and fire-fighting services, and the
like . . . They are a new type, what might be called the
organised militant citizen. And the whole circumstances of
their war-time life favour a sharply democratic outlook. Men
and women with a gift for leadership now turn up in unexpected places. The new ordeals blast away the old shame.
Britain, which in the years immediately before this war was
rapidly losing such democratic virtues as it possessed, is now
being bombed and burned into democracy.'

'Comradeship' would perhaps be a better word than 'democracy'. This was a pleasing bonus for the hard-pressed citizens
of the lonely island. Lots of the comradeship wore off during the post-war troubles, but by no means all.

4

During the twilight war there was nothing to engender this
new comradeship, except for those in the navy and the merchant marine. For the most part, those on shore could only
complain and seek amusement. They lived in a world which
was not at peace but which did not seem to be at war.

Except for Churchill at the Admiralty, even the Cabinet

looks somnolent in retrospect. In the autumn of 1939, after an unprecedented drought, Leo Amery suggested to the Air Minister that incendiary bombs on the Black Forest would destroy immense stores of German munitions. He was answered peevishly: 'Are you aware it is private property? Why, you will be asking me to bomb Essen next.' This sounds like Lewis Carroll; it was the Rt Hon. Kingsley Wood.

If the civilian head of the Royal Air Force was still fussing about the private property of Germans, how could the people of England remember that the life of their country was at stake? Until Dunkirk like a fire-bell in the night roused them from slumber, they made small effort to put the nation or themselves on a war footing.

Euan Wallace, unlike some Ministers, knew that bad times would soon be coming. So some of his old friends perplexed him. On November 18, 1939, he wrote: 'Shooting at Blenheim . . . the attitude of the people to whom the war has made no difference at all . . . inclined to resent slower trains . . . and the fact that the added money for some of the more important races next season was likely to be diminished . . . They all had their own valets and appeared to have no difficulty in motoring from place to place in order to shoot four or five days a week.'

The Minister recorded a happier note on April 16, 1940: 'The effect of the invasion of Norway has been to stimulate an interest in the war.' The Minister can be forgiven his acidity. His job had been to organise the evacuation of hundreds of thousands of people, from all the great towns, on the outbreak of war. The planning had been exact. A fair percentage of the people to be evacuated agreed to this distasteful uprooting. The great 'move' took place, and then nothing happened; instead of a torrent of bombs, there came a few false alarms. The evacuees streamed home again: children, mothers, the lot. 'I am quite convinced', wrote the Minister on October 23, 'that unless we have really heavy air-raids in London, there will be few children left in the reception areas by Christmas.'[11] Knowing that the air-raids would come when the fallow days of the war ended, he must have felt this pause, this weird inaction, as almost a personal insult by Hitler. His planning was undone. The job would have to be rushed through later, helter-skelter, when the bombs began falling.

Accompanied by much recrimination, this is what happened —first in London and later in the other large towns as the Luftwaffe spread its wings and 'rained contagion' over the British Isles. Leaving aside the old and the useless who, if they had money, found themselves a safe hotel in a remote valley, four million people were evacuated, or re-evacuated, at some time during the war. During the first three days of the war 1,493,391 people had been moved.

Because of the absurd estimates of air-raid casualties which the Government had been given (and had no means of checking) some 140,000 sick people were prematurely discharged from hospitals to make room for the expected rush of newly wounded. More than 7,000 tubercular patients were sent home to spread disease. Many of the best nurses and doctors were kept idly awaiting the patients whom the Luftwaffe did not provide. The first test of this vast preparation came after Dunkirk, when 32,000 casualties from the British Expeditionary Force were received.

Richard Titmuss comments: 'Those who suffered in the early months of the war—and at other periods during 1940–1945— were not air-raid casualties, nor were they men in uniform. They were the sick, the diseased, the old, the very young and mothers—all those who were denied hospital room . . . After six years of war, after the blitz of 1940–41, the later bombings, the flying bombs and the rockets, the total number of civilian air-raid casualties treated in hospitals from beginning to end was roughly forty per cent less than the number of sick people turned out of hospitals in about two days in September 1939.'

[11] As early as September 7 he noted: 'People are now reported to be coming home.'

This sounds like a mad blunder; but who could tell before the blitz began? The figures from the small-scale German raids during the first war, the figures from Guernica during the Spanish war, the opinions of 'experts' like Lindbergh who had seen everything the Luftwaffe had to show, in the air and on the factory floor, all seemed to predict an extreme slaughter. Only a wizard, or a rash and stubborn man, could have said 'Pooh to all that'.

In any case, no such pushing-about had ever been attempted in the past. And it will not be attempted in the future: a four-minute warning is inadequate.

B. S. Johnson, who has collected the reminiscences of some of his fellow-evacuees, admits that the plan saved lives. 'The figure', he writes, 'of 60,595 civilians who died in the bombing of Britain would certainly have been increased without evacuation. Whether the number of lives saved was worth the psychological damage to several millions of school children is one of those unanswerable questions of balance which war throws up. The full cost of this evacuated generation's suffering has yet to be counted: we have not yet come fully to power, and the next thirty years will be ours. Those who ordered our saving and suffering are already dead or dying.'

Mr Johnson does not sound pleased. Most of the contributors to his book do not sound pleased. Adults could escape evacuation if they chose ('except insofar as it may be necessary for military or other special reasons to require persons to leave some limited area'); but children were trapped if their parents wished them to leave. Hence, the sense of being abandoned, which they recall even thirty years later.

'We weren't to know this day would end in betrayal,' writes one who was kindly and efficiently transferred from his home to his foster home; but he did not want to be transferred, and nobody had asked him. 'What followed at the reception centre', wrote another, 'was like an auction sale.'

Most of the memories are hostile; but here and there comes a friendly note, or a note of resignation. 'The war to us was the way things were. I was seven, Peter and Wendy six. Peace was something our parents wanted' . . . 'For us "vaccies" there was no cordial welcome from the local kids. All they extended to us was a fast-moving fist between the eyes' . . . 'We were city mongrels, gathered from the streets, feeling hopelessly lost' . . . 'I suppose it might be natural for a child to be afraid of open spaces after having come from a place like London. My Yorkshire grandparents' farm scared me . . . There were too many things with which I could never become familiar' . . . (Other children list goats and cows as forever fearsome; also horses, which were 'free and strangely savage') . . . 'As the train left Bromley South Station I watched the shuttling slums with a sudden desperate love . . . These were my people, my sights and sounds. I loved every scruffy plane tree, every blatant cinema, every hoarding shouting *News of the World* and *Lifebuoy Soap*' . . . 'Unhappiness can bring its own blackout; when I visited that village (in Devonshire) many years later I did not find one building, street or vista that I recognised' . . .

One man, looking back, finds the whole concept of saving the children inhumane. If an eight-year-old boy, who is being parted from his mother and sent to live with strangers, asks 'why', he should never be told that this is to save him from danger. 'This terrifyingly implies that the mother is exposed to that danger from which he is being protected; and the thought of his mother being killed and him being left was far greater agony of mind than the possibility of injury or death to himself.'

On the other hand, a girl who was fourteen in 1940 and whose life in Canning Town (London) and in foster homes had not been idyllic, wrote in 1968: 'I thank God I was evacuated: not because I avoided danger . . . but because it changed my way of thinking, it made me love the country . . . I found another family whom I really loved, and still do.'

The most pleasing memory is that of a ten-year-old boy who was sent to his grandmother's house in the Cotswolds: 'When the church bells rang out in the night and we thought the invasion had at last begun, I remember seeing the wife of the chimney-sweep sharpening her carving knife on the stone sill of her cottage.' Carving Germans was at least as practical as hitting them on the head with beer bottles.

Mr Titmuss sums up the unhappy side of evacuation: 'Town and country met each other in a critical mood. The wartime guests of the country were further aggrieved when, in many areas, they were walked or paraded around while householders took their pick . . . One boy likened it to "a cattle show" for farmers picked strong-looking lads, and the presentable, nicely dressed children were quickly chosen.'

5

Aside from the Government-sponsored evacuation, the chief differences between the English and the French during the grumbling period of the twilight war were that discipline was better in the small British Expeditionary Force than in the huge French army, and that the war was somewhat enlivened for the civilian public in Great Britain because there was much ado at sea.

On the first day of the war the liner *Athenia* was sunk, with a number of Americans on board. This annoyed Ambassador Kennedy, who thought his fellow-citizens should be inviolate and who was trying to persuade Washington that the Germans were by nature friendly. A fortnight later the aircraft carrier *Courageous* was sunk in the Bristol Channel. This annoyed the British who felt that while the Germans might maraud in the wastes of oceans they should not be seen in home waters.

Worse was to come. On October 14 a U-boat crept into Scapa Flow and sank *Royal Oak*, a battleship, at her moorings. This was impossible: but the war was to be full of impossibilities. Some 800 men were lost. When Mr Churchill explained the disaster to the House of Commons, he referred to the heroism of the German officer, Lieutenant Prien.[12] Euan Wallace, who was present, wrote in his diary: 'It was characteristic of the House of Commons to give a decided cheer when Winston paid tribute to the daring and navigational skill of the attacker.'

Hitler, had he been present, might have wondered. He might even have shivered over this brief glimpse at the inexplicable people he had challenged.

Thereafter, the naval news improved. In December *Graf Spee* (a 'pocket battleship' with six 11-inch guns and a speed of 26 knots) was cornered in Uruguay and forced to blow herself up. In February, 1940, the heart-warming and illegal boarding of the *Altmark,* in Norwegian waters, released 299 British prisoners and reminded the public that the navy, at least, was not being lulled into slumber.

Then came the invasion of Norway, which 'stimulated an interest in the war'. On April 4 the doomed Chamberlain made his silliest speech. The Germans had wasted their chance in September, he said, when they were better prepared than the British. Now they had lost their advantage. Hitler had 'missed the bus'.

On April 8 the Allies began mining Norwegian waters, to delay iron-ore shipments from northern Sweden. Churchill had urged this on the Cabinet as early as September, 1939. He said that such a minefield would be 'of the highest importance in crippling the enemy's war industry'. The Foreign Office vetoed this violation of neutrality. Churchill writes: 'I continued . . . to press my point by every means and on all occasions.'

According to Liddell Hart, Hitler would have preferred to keep Norway neutral; but the Germans were ready to move with startling speed when the route for their iron-ore was

---

[12] By the time he was at last sunk by a British destroyer, Prien had dispatched 200,000 tons of Allied shipping.

threatened. Churchill was right in judging the importance of that route.

The day after the mine-laying began, Hitler took Denmark and invaded Norway. The French and the British responded. Terrible events were soon to distract them from their brief troubles in the Arctic. Yet in this frustrating come-and-go the Royal Navy once more reassured the British people. Years later Churchill wrote: 'In their desperate grapple with the British navy, the Germans ruined their own, such as it was, for the impending climax.'[13]

The Norway campaign left the Germans with one 8-inch-gun cruiser, two light cruisers and four destroyers plus fifty-six U-boats. Many of these losses would quickly be repaired, and the Germans were building some mighty vessels; but, as Churchill noted, 'the German navy was no longer a factor in the supreme issue of the invasion of Britain'.

The British campaign in Norway has been dismissed as a costly mistake. Early in May the *Manchester Guardian* used it as an excuse to attack eight months of drifting: 'If we look back over these eight months, with problem after problem misman-aged or neglected, with speech after speech revealing the same lack of grasp and imagination, we are driven to the con-clusion that we are facing the greatest crisis in our history with a Government weaker than any Government that has made war since Addington faced Napoleon . . . What is needed is a Government that can organise the nation's strength, touch its imagination, command its spirit of self-sacrifice, impose burdens fearlessly on all classes, put the war before everything else, look ahead with cool and deliberate courage.'

The American Ambassador, Joseph Kennedy, told the For-eign Secretary and the Minister of Information that England was lost and degenerate: the armed forces, labour, everybody. He added (which was not true) that the United States' at-

---

[13] The Germans admit to losing one heavy cruiser, two light cruisers, ten destroyers, one torpedo boat and six U-boats.

tachés were agreed that England would lose the war. Lord Reith and Lord Halifax were as little likely to be disturbed by such remarks as any two men alive; but Kennedy's total defeatism was no help to those in America who were preaching that Britain would never fall.

Blundering and humiliating as it was on land, the naval results of the Norwegian campaign may have helped to frustrate the invasion of Britain in the summer of 1940. How can a world-conqueror without a navy invade an island of seafarers? Goering thought he had an answer; but it did not work.

Another possible answer would have been a sufficient supply of U-boats and of magnetic mines when the war started. This the Germans did not have, which is odd in view of the lessons of the First World War. When Admiral Tirpitz launched the submarine campaign which brought America into the war in 1917, he could have starved England before American help was of any value if Germany had possessed an extra hundred U-boats. He almost did it anyway. But Hitler, luckily, knew nothing about the sea except that it made him sick. So he challenged the long-time masters of the oceans with fifty-six U-boats, hoping to have a hundred in a few months.[14]

Admiral Doenitz had told Hitler before the war that if Great Britain used convoys on all her trade-routes he would need 300 submarines to starve her. We now know he could have done the job. Even with his pitiful fifty-six (only eighteen of which were large enough to work in the Atlantic) and with the help of airplanes and surface raiders, he had sunk over 420,000 tons of Allied and neutral shipping by the end of 1939.

Throughout 1940 the shortage of U-boats again saved Britain. Had she faced wide-spread malnutrition while fighting the Battle of Britain and enduring the subsequent blitz, she must have perished.

[14] By February, 1940, sixteen U-boats had been sunk and nine had been built.

In the winter of 1941 the United States moved her 'Security Zone', which was patrolled by the United States navy, from 60° West to 28° West—an enormous benefit to British convoys. Then American marines took over from British forces in Iceland and the American navy guarded her shipments to Britain as far as Reykjavik. Also British merchantships and warships were refitting in American yards. None of this sufficed, and the terror of the U-boats grew. Even after the United States was in the war (or perhaps because the United States was in the war with a navy largely preoccupied with Japan), Great Britain was in mortal danger; at one time within three months of starvation. The winter of 1942–43 saw the climax of this horror. Then at last, in May 1943, came victory in the Atlantic.

Everything was done to conceal the facts at the time. How many people in this vulnerable island know, today, that while they were celebrating 'the end of the beginning' in North Africa they were close to being beaten at sea?

By August, 1942, Doenitz had his 300 submarines, about half of them operational at any given time. The British had meanwhile perfected a radar set which the U-boats could not intercept; but this again did not suffice. In November, 1942, the Germans sank 637,907 tons of shipping. The silent, unrecorded Battle of the Atlantic had become at least as critical as the Battle of Britain. In January, 1943, a convoy from Trinidad to Gibraltar lost seven out of nine tankers. By this time Britain was 'eating her own tail'.

As Admiral Morison reminds us, 'One of the worst winters on record was lashing the Western Ocean . . . During most of the winter the weather was so foul that long-range land-based planes could not fly, and several of those that did never returned.'

March was the crisis. Liddell Hart quotes the Admiralty as saying that 'the Germans never came so near to disrupting communication between the New World and the Old as in the first twenty days of March, 1943'.

By April the tide was turning and by May it had turned.

Thirty-eight U-boats were sunk during that month and only twenty-six were built. By July the Allies were building more merchant ships than the Germans could sink. The U-boat was reduced to an inconvenience.

Nothing succeeds like success. Toward the end of 1943 Portugal at last allowed the Allies to base anti-submarine planes on the Azores. Such planes already flew from Greenland, Iceland, Newfoundland and the British Isles; but there was still a 'black pit' in mid-Atlantic where convoys lacked air protection. The Azores were the answer. Once they were available the Germans had lost the Atlantic. And, as Field-Marshal Rommel realised, they had also lost the war.

Among Rommel's reflections on his campaigns, written while at home recovering from his injuries in Normandy, he comments: 'Some hope did remain as long as our submarines were able to maintain their mastery of the Atlantic, for the greatest production of tanks, guns and vehicles would have availed America nothing if she could not have carried them across the seas. But this "Battle of the Atlantic", which in all probability decided the whole war, was soon lost by us with frightful casualties among our U-boats. All else was dependent on this fact, and we were now doomed to inevitable defeat at any place which was accessible to the Anglo-American transport fleets.'[15]

I have transgressed the time-period of my book to outline this story because, as Rommel says, everything depended on its outcome and it seems to be little remembered. The U-boat was the one weapon which might have made useless the valour of Britain in 1940–41. During all those crisis-months I was at the American Embassy in London, on loan from the navy. Thus I watched the dismaying figures, while my friends were discussing the conference at Casablanca and the doc-

---

[15] A dramatic account of the Battle of the Atlantic, by a U-boat commander who chanced to survive, is *Iron Coffins* by Herbert A. Werner, London 1969. The Appendices give exact figures for U-boat losses and sinkings throughout the war.

trine of 'unconditional surrender'. I wondered whether they knew whose surrender was imminent.

I was not alone in my perturbation. 'The only thing that ever really frightened me during the war', wrote Churchill, 'was the U-boat peril . . . Compared with this there was no value in brave armies ready to leap upon the invader, or in a good plan for desert warfare. The high and faithful spirit of the people counted for nought in this bleak domain.' As Belloc put it: 'All that which concerns the sea is profound and final.'

Early in the war Germany's magnetic mines, had they been abundant and backed by big manufacturing plants, might have done the job at which the U-boats failed; but again the supply was inadequate. In the autumn of 1939 one of these mines was recovered from a mudbank off the Essex coast so the navy learned how the thing worked. Ships could be de-magnetized by girdling them with an electric cable; but mine-sweeping became perilous. The Germans kept changing the electronic rules of 'the thing' while the British struggled to out-think the out-thinkers.

In the autumn of 1940 came the acoustic mine, detonated by the sound of a ship's propellers. Two 'acoustics' were found in the mudflats of the Bristol Channel and a way was devised to detonate them at a safe distance; but again new designs meant that ever new counter-measures had to be invented in this secret war between the men of science.

The public was told as little as possible about mine-dangers, since the public could do nothing to help; but the dangers remained great. Churchill wrote: 'It is well to ponder this side of the naval war. In the event a significant proportion of our whole war effort had to be devoted to combatting the mine. A vast output of material and money was diverted from other tasks, and many thousand men risked their lives night and day in the minesweepers alone. The peak figure was reached in June, 1944, when nearly 60,000 men were thus employed.'

Again, had Hitler thought like a sailor, had he thought of

the problems of life on an island which produced (at the start of the war) less than half its necessary food, he might have begun with huge supplies of mines and with many factories to replace them. He might have crippled England by the time he was ready to overrun France.

And yet—was it simply ignorance which made him neglect the advice of Doenitz and the common sense which must have told him that if mines were to be effective they must be over-abundant? Or was it the strange ambivalence of his feelings toward England? With half his mind he wanted to fight the English, with whom (again with half his mind) he thought he could make friends. From time to time, in the early days, he clearly believed it was a mistake to be at war with England and that the English would see the mistake if he could only explain. A few days before granting the armistice to France, Hitler told Goering: 'The war is finished. I'll come to an understanding with England.' The English, after all, were honorary Aryans. (Hitler forgot about the Celts on the fringes.)

He also forgot what he had written in *Mein Kampf*.

'The British nation will therefore be considered as the most valuable ally in the world as long as it can be counted on to show that brutality and tenacity in its government, as well as in the spirit of the broad masses, which enables it to carry through to victory any struggle that it once enters upon, no matter how long such a struggle may last or however great the sacrifice that may be necessary or whatever the means that have to be employed; and all this even though the actual military equipment at hand may be utterly inadequate when compared with that of other nations.'

This could almost be Hitler's obituary. It does not sound like the description of people who would 'come to an understanding' merely because they had lost an Ally.

In another part of *Mein Kampf* Hitler was criticising past German policy. 'If European soil was wanted,' he wrote, 'by

and large it could be had only at the expense of Russia . . .
For such a policy as this there was but one ally in Europe—
England. Only with England covering our rear could we have
begun a new German migration. No sacrifice should have
been too great in winning England's friendship. We should
have given up all thought of colonies and sea power and
avoided all competition with British industry.'

He did not take his own advice; but he was clearly perplexed by England.

The same problem of a divided mind arises over Hitler's
famous *Halt Befehl* of May 24, the order which kept Guderian's tanks from rushing on to Dunkirk and killing or captur-
ing 300,000 troops. After the war Field-Marshal Rundstedt
testified: 'I recommended to the Supreme Command that my
five panzer divisions be immediately sent into the town and
thereby completely destroy the retreating English . . . I was
expressly forbidden to send any of my troops closer than ten
kilometres from Dunkirk . . . I sat outside the town, watching
the English escape, while my tanks and infantry were pro-
hibited from moving.'

Liddell Hart agrees that Rundstedt could have finished the
British Expeditionary Force. 'After his tanks had overrun the
North of France and cut off the British army from its base,'
he writes, 'Hitler held them up just as they were about
to sweep into Dunkirk . . . His action preserved the British
forces when nothing else could have saved them . . . Thereby
he produced his own ultimate downfall.'

Such was the true 'miracle of Dunkirk'; but why? Had Hitler
accepted Goering's boast that the Luftwaffe alone could do
the job? Was he worried about the fifty per cent of break-
downs in the Panzer Corps? The tanks could quickly be repaired for the Battle of the Somme; but ever since the first war
Hitler had an evil memory of marshy Flanders and he may
have thought that by pursuing the British into these badlands
he might lose his chance of annihilating the French. Or was

it again his equivocal feelings about the British, his half-belief and half-wish that he could 'come to an understanding with the English'?[16]

The Hitler of *Mein Kampf* wrote of 'the brutality and tenacity in its government, as well as in the spirit of the broad masses,' once England goes to war. He had recently had excuse for thinking that these qualities might have weakened or at least that they might not be displayed against himself and his Nazis. As Albert Soral noted, the English turn easily from lukewarm lethargy to cold ferocity. The lethargy must have impressed Hitler during the days of Chamberlain. Geoffrey Dawson, the editor of *The Times,* gave a splendid example of this trait. He acted as foreign editor as well as editor of his paper. He remade the overseas despatches of his correspondents until they fitted his own hopes and fears. He described his methods: 'I did my utmost, night after night, to keep out of the paper anything that might hurt their [the Germans'] susceptibilities.'

Dawson was everything that would impress a German Ambassador: Fellow of All Souls, intimate friend of Halifax and Chamberlain, head of a newspaper which was wrongly thought to speak for the Government. Why shouldn't Hitler think he had friends in England, and that once the little misunderstandings over Poland and France were solved (by the destruction of both countries) he and Chamberlain could get on famously?

And what was he to make of Lloyd George, an important name to anyone who had fought in the First World War? In September, 1936, Lloyd George went to see Hitler in Germany. Kingsley Martin reports. 'He was completely bowled over by Hitler . . . He called him "the greatest German of the age".' And when he returned home he wrote articles for the Beaverbrook press in which he praised the Nazi régime and

[16] Or could he have believed what he told Kleist who reproached Hitler for *Halt Befehl:* 'The British won't come back in this war.'

stated: 'The Germans have definitely made up their minds never to quarrel with us again.'[17]

All this belied the temper of the British people. All this was of the past once Churchill came to power. Toward the end of the escape from Dunkirk, Churchill spoke to a group of his Cabinet Ministers. 'Of course,' he remarked in passing, 'whatever happens at Dunkirk, we shall fight on.' The relief, the delight which was expressed pleased the Old Man Valorous. 'I was sure', he wrote in *Their Finest Hour*, 'that every Minister was ready to be killed quite soon, and have all his family and possessions destroyed, rather than give in. In this they represented the House of Commons and almost all the people.'

Later, referring to the same dark days, Churchill wrote: 'Future generations may deem it noteworthy that the supreme question of whether we should fight on alone never found a place upon the War Cabinet agenda. It was taken for granted and as a matter of course by these men of all parties in the State, and we were much too busy to waste time upon such unreal, academic issues.'

On June 17, with France already seeking an armistice, Churchill broadcast: 'What has happened in France makes no difference to our actions and purpose. We have become the sole champions now in arms to defend the world cause. We shall do our best to be worthy of this high honour . . . We are sure that in the end all will come right.'

The next day Churchill spoke to Parliament: 'Hitler knows that he will have to break us in this island or lose the war . . . If we fail, then the whole world, including the United States, including all that we have known and cared for, will sink into the abyss of a new Dark Age, made more sinister, and perhaps more protracted, by the lights of perverted science.'

[17] When the war began, Lloyd George soon became a defeatist, a 'Pétain' as Churchill called him. 'It was said', wrote Kingsley Martin, 'that he was prepared to act as "Britain's last card", that is, the man on whom the burden would fall of making the best terms he could for England if we were compelled to capitulate.'

Finally, in a clairvoyant message to General Smuts on June 19, Churchill said: 'I see only one way through now, to wit, that Hitler should attack this country, and in doing so break his air weapon.'

This is now on the record. It contrasts strangely with the words which in those same days were spoken at Bordeaux. And it contrasts strangely with the mood in the United States where all but a few were stunned by the defeat of France and thought that Churchill was bluffing. Years later, musing over the stupidity of world opinion in June, 1940, Churchill wrote: 'Foreigners who do not understand the temper of the British race all over the globe when its blood is up might suppose that they [Churchill's speeches] were only a bold front, set up as a good prelude for peace negotiations . . . Not every nation, while quite alone and as it seemed abandoned, would have courted the horrors of invasion and disdained a fair chance of peace for which many plausible excuses could be presented.'

Hitler was among the foreigners who did not understand the temper of the British race. He hoped he was fighting Geoffrey Dawsons and was annoyed to find that he was fighting Churchills. He did not seem to know, as Ludendorff had known instinctively a generation earlier, that no war in which Britain is involved can ever be won until the British themselves have been defeated.

Preparing for his last-hope offensive in March, 1918, Ludendorff summed up: he could use thirty-five fresh divisions and a thousand new heavy guns; but that was the end. No other offensive was possible; therefore, no use going for the French: 'We must beat the British.' Hitler took a different view when he stopped his tanks outside Dunkirk, and no good came of it for him.

When the British had at last made clear that they were implacable, Hitler felt let down. He repeated the ancient epithet, *Albion perfide*, which his own propagandists had used effectively in France. *Albion* was not being *perfide*; it was merely being English. With many dissensions among themselves, the English had agreed to eat humble pie and to make the utmost concessions to gain that 'piece of paper' at Munich. Perhaps Hitler hoped they could be bullied. They could not. Hitler had misinformed Goering: he never had a chance, after Poland, of 'coming to an understanding with the English'. He thought they had misled him; they knew, finally, that he had lied to them and made fools of them. This they did not like.

IV
Invasion?

1

In 1923, as a pleasant change from brooding over the Treaty
of Versailles, the Wehrmacht produced a detailed plan for the
conquest of the world. When Franz Halder became Chief of
the German Central Staff in 1938 he studied this plan. It did
not tell him the one thing he wanted to know in 1940: how to
invade England.

Major-General Fuller, commenting on Hitler's audacity,
wrote: 'While gazing at the map of the British Empire he had
overlooked the Strait of Dover. If its crossing was an insuper-
able problem, he should not have gone to war. If it were not,
then he should have prepared to solve it before launching the
war.' This is true. The most important non-event of 1940 was
the invasion of Britain. Yet General Fuller was a little hard on
Hitler in view of the many predecessors who had made the
same mistake.

The first serious attempt at invasion since the Norman Conquest was made during the last years of Henry VIII, stemming
from his meaningless and unproductive wars with France.
The French had built a huge armada of 200 ships, carrying
60,000 troops, with which to seize the Isle of Wight and invade
southern England. Meanwhile a Franco-Scottish force was to
attack from the north.

The winds and tides were unpropitious when the 200 ships
headed for Portsmouth. The French, under Francis I, landed
a few hundred men for a few hours on the Isle of Wight and a
few hundred more pillaged the coast of Sussex. Then the
winds took over. Landings became impossible and evacua-
tions difficult. Then plague broke out among the 60,000 tight-
packed troops who had been at sea for almost four weeks.
The French king recalled his infested ships to Le Havre. He,
too, had not informed himself about the currents and the
tides and the winds and the shifting sands of the English
Channel.

Peace was declared on June 7, 1546, the year before Henry
died. The purpose of the war seems doubtful to the latest
biographer of Henry VIII: but surely one result should have
been to cry, 'Beware the coasts of England!' to all future invaders.

The same weather and the same coasts and the same ignorance ruined the Spanish Armada in 1588.

When France joined the American Colonists in their War
of Independence in 1778, and when Spain joined the coalition
the next year, the invasion of England seemed possible. Fifty
thousand troops were assembled at Le Havre and Cherbourg,
to land between Portsmouth and the Isle of Wight. The
French and Spanish fleets, eluding the British, joined off
Finistère. 'Sixty-six great ships', writes Admiral Richmond, 'and
a mass of frigates and lesser vessels appeared in the mouth of
the Channel where the British had no more than fifty ships.'
Superior seamanship, and a knowledge of the quirks and
dangers of these narrow seas, gave victory to the smaller but
more nimble British fleet. 'Nimble' is Admiral Richmond's
word, and nimbleness was the reward for hundreds of years
of experience in these strange waters.

Then came Napoleon. He, too, gathered his armies on the
French coast. 'Let us be masters of the Straits for twelve
hours,' he said, 'and we shall be masters of the world.' With
the entry of the Spanish fleet in 1805, the problem shifted from

little ships and the invasion ports to the outer oceans. If the English ships-of-the-line could be defeated, Napoleon could control his Straits for as long as he chose. Trafalgar was the answer.

Ever since Roman days the winds had been helpful to England, which lies in the zone of the Westerlies where the winds are more likely to blow toward France than away from her. The coming of steam changed all that. Wellington warned that unless the fleet was enlarged 'we are not safe for a week after the declaration of war'.

In 1899 the French were furious over the Fashoda incident of the previous year and the British were drifting into the Boer war. A brilliant Frenchman prepared plans for a landing craft which was practical and which could even have been used in Hitler's war. Most of the problems of landing on the 'invasion coast' of England are faced and dealt with in theory, and in theory a few hundred of these craft could land 160,000 men, with artillery, in a night.

A pity for Hitler that he never read the *Revue de Deux Mondes* of March, 1899. No one thereafter understood the multiple problems of the landing craft, until the Americans grappled with the Japanese in the South Pacific.

Yet in spite of the precedents, and what might have been learned from them, I repeat the most important non-event of 1940 was the invasion of Britain. The thought, the decisions and indecisions, the improvisation and hard work which were lavished upon this un-invasion would have sufficed for a major campaign. Had the German plan (or lack of plan) succeeded, Europe must have perished, for Hitler would have been undistracted during his war on Russia. When France fell most of the world expected this invasion to follow fast and to overwhelm the defenceless island.[1]

---

[1] As early as June 6, just after Dunkirk, the British Ambassador in Madrid reported that 'nine Spaniards out of ten believe that Hitler will win the war in three weeks'.

'Within six weeks [of May 10]' wrote Churchill, 'we were to find ourselves alone, almost disarmed, with triumphant Germany and Italy at our throats, with the whole of Europe in Hitler's power, and Japan glowering on the other side of the globe.' The British people must have felt that by magic the turbulent Channel would protect them, or how could 97 per cent of the population expect to win the war? 'Never has a great nation been so naked before her foes' was the view of the Prime Minister. Yet the people were not frightened; they were cheerful.

Peter Fleming writes: 'The historian can only record that the British, when their last ally was poleaxed on their doorstep, became both gayer and more serene than they had been at any time since the overture to Munich struck up in 1937.' And he quotes Margery Allingham who found that perilous summer 'more entirely satisfying than any other piece of life which I at least have ever experienced'. Recently A. J. P. Taylor has testified to the 'enormous exuberance during the Battle of Britain. Anyone looking back must confess that the summer of 1940 was not only the most exciting, but also the gayest, time of his life.' So it seemed to many of my friends: a mysterious but enviable mood. By comparison, 'aiding the Allies' in the United States was a joyless comedown.

The men in command did not wholly share the civilian gaiety, although General Ismay told his wife that, even without France, Britain's chances of survival were 'three to one on'. Twice in the last two months the Germans had taken the Allies by surprise and made them look slow and stupid: first in Norway and then on the River Meuse. Both times the Germans had done with ease what the Allies had assumed to be impossible. What other tricks had they prepared, what other deadly and unforeseeable plans for the disarmed island? The people were in fact right to feel gay, for there were no such plans; but those responsible for the nation's life (and thus for all good and hopeful things everywhere) had to assume that something fearful, new and wicked was about to be revealed.

On July 14 Churchill broadcast to the British people, telling them his worries and his hopes. His worries were about invasion. 'We have seen', he said, 'how Hitler prepared in scientific detail the plans for destroying the neighbour countries of Germany. He had his plans for Poland and his plans for Norway . . . He had his plans all worked out for the peaceful, trustful Dutch; and, of course, for the Belgians. We have seen how the French were undermined and overthrown. We may therefore be sure that there *is* a plan—perhaps built up over years—for destroying Great Britain, which after all has the honour to be his main and foremost enemy.'

Churchill then gave his audience the quaint reassurance that whereas it had been necessary to keep the army in France 'we now have it all at home'. He did not add that its chief armament was American rifles and machine-guns left over from the First World War. He did add that every inch of soil would be defended. 'The vast mass of London itself, fought street by street, could easily devour an entire hostile army . . . It is necessary', he concluded, 'to inform our people of our intentions and thus to reassure them.'

This ominous discourse did in fact 'reassure them'. This is exactly what they wanted to hear: no nonsense about an 'open city', like Paris. No thought of anything but war. And the one gloomy note, that Hitler must have *some* plan for getting at Britain was not true. Hitler had nothing new to reveal: only the usual Hitlerian muddle-think about England and the usual boastfulness from Goering about the destruction of the Royal Air Force. Yet we should recall Maitland's warning to historians: 'It is very hard to remember that events now long in the past were once in the future.' To feel for the leaders of Britain in June, 1940, we must read ourselves into their anxiety and ask: 'What else have the Germans got ready—prepared and organised to the last inch?'

Because of the fearsomeness of that question, and the impossibility of finding an answer except in retrospect, the stubborn belligerence of the Cabinet is impressive. 'There was a white glow,' wrote Churchill, 'over-powering, sublime, which ran through our island from end to end.'

Isaiah Berlin agrees, but adds that Churchill had much to do with creating the glow: 'So hypnotic was the force of his words, so strong his faith, that by the sheer intensity of his eloquence he bound his spell upon them until it seemed to them that he was indeed speaking what was in their hearts and minds. Doubtless it was there; but largely dormant until he had awoken it within them.'

Out of this spirit came the splendid improvisations, the creation of 'the people's war', which soon made invasion a lost cause unless Fighter Command could be destroyed.

On June 5, the day after the end of 'Dunkirk', only one German had a plan for action. The British had lost their arms, and the men of the ex-B.E.F. were also worn down by their labours. Inspector-General Erhard Milch of the Luftwaffe tried to persuade Goering to invade that day, by air, capture a foot-hold and a few coastal airfields, turn the Stukas loose to create Chaos and Old Night and then ferry a few regiments across in the dark by every available ship. Fighter Command was down to about twenty-seven squadrons. This wild adventure— which Goering disregarded and which Hitler would have vetoed since he was waiting for England to make peace—was Germany's best chance for invasion.

The deaths, and the astonishment, and the howling Stukas would presumably have left the men of Kent unperturbed; but Milch was right. This was the propitious moment. Even had Goering finally won the Battle of Britain, September was too late for landlubbers to attempt the treacherous Channel.

In order to be ready for a proper invasion in June or in July (not a terror-raid such as Milch advised), the Germans should have started mass-producing troop landing-craft and tank landing-craft by the time of the collapse of Poland. Even the seafaring nations, in those early days, did not know the importance and the awkwardness of landing-craft. The Americans in the Pacific, the Allies in the Mediterranean and Normandy, were to learn the need for masses of these cross-tempered machines. Hitler's little invasion-barges, most of which were to be towed, look pathetic in retrospect. Had any of the High Command in Germany ever tried to sail a small boat in the Channel, even in a day of 'friendly' weather, the thought of towing canal-boats in September would have been abandoned.

Since Hitler had no landing-craft and no troops trained in amphibious warfare, one can say today with some confidence that the Germans had at last 'missed the bus' unless Fighter Command could be obliterated in high summer: July or August at the latest.

'Obliterated' is a big word. Peter Wykeham reminds us what total control of the air meant on D-Day 1944: the same control which Goering had promised Hitler. During the six weeks before D-Day the Luftwaffe sent 125 planes toward England to find out what was happening and where it was planned to happen. None of them reached the coast. 'In the same period the Allies flew 4,700 photographic reconnaissances over Europe.' And on D-Day itself the Allies had '9,210 aircraft directly concerned with Overlord[2] without counting the strategic bombers'.

Granted that the Germans had an army defending the west coast of their *Festung Europa*—whereas the British had noth-ing during June, 1940—the magnitude of the Allied air supremacy in 1944 is a guide to what Goering needed in 1940 if Hitler's river-boats were to be towed across that Channel.

How could the people of England know that Hitler's armies when they reached the Channel had no plans and no equip-ment for invasion and that the Fuehrer was waiting with mounting folly for a British offer of peace? While wait-ing he magnified his threats, to the amusement rather than the terror of the British. His Luftwaffe practised bombing raids

[2] Code name for Allied invasion of Europe, June, 1944.

hither and yon, thus helping Fighter Command to learn the German weaknesses. Finally, the barges and the trawlers and other unsuitable craft began assembling at the invasion ports from Rotterdam to Etaples, and German soldiers began learning how to get in and out of salt water.

They were too late. Hitler had not issued his half-hearted directive for the invasion of England until July 16: 'Since England, despite her militarily hopeless situation, still shows no sign of willingness to come to terms, I have decided to prepare a landing operation against England, and if necessary to carry it out.'

That is no clarion call, and since neither the army nor the navy approved there was at first no hurry about preparing. Even Hitler did not press for speed because he could not believe that England meant what Churchill kept saying. As early as May 24 the Fuehrer told Rundstedt that the British Empire was useful, that only the Japanese and the Americans would benefit if it was broken and that Germany merely wanted a free hand on the Continent. So why should these mad islanders go on fighting? William Shirer reports that in midsummer 1940 everybody in Berlin, especially in the Government, 'was confident that the war was as good as over'.

Yet when the King of Sweden suggested the possibility of peace discussions he got a dusty answer. Nothing of the sort could be considered, said the British Government, until 'effective guarantees by deeds, not words, should be forthcoming from Germany which would ensure the restoration of the free and independent life of Czechoslovakia, Poland, Norway, Denmark, Holland, Belgium and above all, France'. Hitler should have reflected that 'a free hand on the Continent', for himself or any other conqueror, was what England had been opposing since the sixteenth century. Add that he had carefully proved to the British that only a fool would believe anything he said, and there seems small reason for surprise at Churchill's intransigence. But the surprise continued, and three days after his directive for invasion 'if necessary' he made another plea for what he called 'peace'.

He appealed to the people of England to revolt, telling them that their leaders would all go to Canada when the German storm broke upon their island, leaving the people to great and unnecessary pain. 'In this hour I feel it my duty before my own conscience to appeal once more to reason and to common sense in Britain as much as elsewhere. I consider myself in a position to make this appeal since I am not the vanquished begging favours but the victor speaking in the name of reason. I see no reason why this war must go on.'

Within the hour, and without prompting from the Government, the B.B.C. had broadcast in German a rejection of this 'offer' which said nothing about the slaves in the conquered countries and merely suggested that the British would be wise to lay down their arms. Again Mr Shirer records stupefaction in Berlin. 'They're crazy', was the consensus among officials.

At last Hitler's divided mind was clarified; his long ambivalence about the British turned to a simple hate. The plans for invasion were pushed, although September was now the earliest date and September must be too late, because of weather, if there were the slightest fight left in the R.A.F.

The in-gathering of the barges and the trawlers became an immense effort, made at an immense sacrifice. Fish from the Baltic, for a nation which was denied all the oceans; the movement of heavy goods throughout the canals of Germany and France; all this was disregarded for the sake of the one dash at England. By September, when the great storms were brewing, Hitler was ready for business; but this was a business he did not understand.

Had he been ready on time, his would have been the worst threat England ever faced. The price of British defeat would have been the loss of everything which could make life worth living in Europe, as Reich-minister Speer has testified.

And what of England herself? In September, when the invasion was at last supposed to be ripe, *Most Secret* draft orders were sent to senior officers in the German army. They were exact. They included the order for civilians to surrender everything anyone could possibly want, plus the usual threat to shoot anybody who so much as made a rude noise. One order, signed in draft by von Brauchitsch, the Commander-in-Chief, has a special interest. Paragraph Four reads: 'The able-bodied male population between the ages of 17 and 45 will, unless the local situation calls for exceptional ruling, be interned and dispatched to the Continent with a minimum of delay.'

Camps were being built in France for the reception of these males. They would join the slave-labour corps, soon to be seven million strong. They would make more weapons to subjugate more continents.

There was no mention in the German orders about the export of British women. Since Hitler thought of them as 'Aryans' they would doubtless be bred to the occupying soldiers so as to increase the master race; concubines rather than slaves. The men were needed on the Continent to work the industries which were to be filched from Britain. The country was to be plundered industrially, stripped bare. These grim plans compare oddly with the 'exuberance', 'gaiety' and 'serenity' felt by the inhabitants of the small, green, rainy island.

On May 1, 1971, Professor W. H. C. Frend of Glasgow University wrote to *The Times* about some of his discoveries as an Editor of the German Foreign Documents. The population of Britain was to be reduced to thirty million people. There was to be a new carve-up of Africa, with a German Empire centred on the Belgian Congo. Since the Africans were among the Nazis' many 'sub-human' groups, the blacks would have lost their last hope.

The plans were not daydreams or wild, inconsequent threats. They had been, or were to be, carried out in detail (with the addition of female slaves when needed) in most of the countries which the Nazis overran. Hence the manpower which, to the world's amazement, helped Speer to increase

Germany's war-production until long after D-Day, long after the airplanes of the Allies roamed at will over the flattened cities of the Reich.

As Professor Galbraith has pointed out this production was not so astounding as it seemed because Hitler's plans for a series of short *blitzkriegs* had not called for heavy production. By the summer of 1942 war production in Germany was about one-quarter of what it had been in 1918. Production for 'total war' began after Stalingrad, some two and a half years after the British had been straining themselves to the edge of exhaustion. And the Germans had not yet made serious use of their women in factories or fields, though they used plenty of other people's women. Speer's increases in production, from 1942 to 1944, sound miraculous: fourfold in weapons and aircraft, threefold in munitions, sixfold in tanks; but the increases 'were multiples of a very small base'.

The Russians suffered most from Speer's plundering of men and women, since the Germans chose to regard Russians as scarcely human. The countless Russian prisoners of war were used for any purpose their owners chose: farm or factory, country house or brothel. Similarly the Jews, who, if able-bodied, were worked to death on a starvation diet in the factories near Auschwitz and similar hells, like so many logs of wood thrown on a fire. These varied forms of servitude—forced labour, brothels, logs of wood, mothers of Aryans etc.—would have been the permanent fate of Europe had Britain faltered.

One reason for the need for all these foreigners was that at first the Nazis made small use of their own women except as baby-makers. Hitler thought that the West's partial emancipation of women was as depraved as its partial democracy. 'Equal rights for women', he said, 'means that they receive the esteem they deserve in the sphere nature has assigned to them . . . Woman has her battlefield too; with each child that she brings into the world for the nation she is fighting her fight on behalf of the nation.'

As Richard Grunberger points out, all this changed after the

battle of Stalingrad. By January, 1943, the Germans had discovered what the British had known from the start, that total
war demands total mobilisation of woman-power. The Gauleiter for labour conscription asked initially for three million
women between seventeen and forty-five years of age. All
mothers with a child under six or two children under fourteen
were to be exempt. Similar call-ups in Great Britain, as we
shall see, produced more than was demanded; but with the
usual Nazi corruption the Germans at first mustered only
900,000 women. Yet by the end of 1944, when the Reich was
tottering, there were 14,500,000 women in the factories. Grunberger comments on 'the basic contradictions that those whom
Nazi rhetoric had destined to the kitchen and the nursery
eventually formed three-fifths of Germany's war-time labour
force.'

The same Albert Speer who had kept the war going for so
many deadly years tried to frustrate Hitler's last ambition,
which was to die in a proper *Götterdämmerung* with Germany
crashing and burning to ruin. In the spring of 1945, not sat-
isfied with the Allies' far from amateurish efforts at bombing
his country into bits, Hitler issued his scorched earth orders.
'The war is lost,' Speer told him on March 15, and Speer was
perhaps the only man in Germany who could survive telling
the truth. 'If the war is lost,' said the Fuehrer, 'then the nation
will also perish.' He gave orders to destroy the country. Power
plants, industries, ports and waterways, highways and railway
rolling stock: all were to burn or to be blown up. Germany
was told to commit suicide.

'There is no reason', said Hitler, 'to consider the basis of even
a most primitive existence any longer . . . It is better to destroy even that, and to destroy it ourselves. The nation has
proved itself weak . . . Those who remain after the battle are
of little value, for the good have fallen.'

This is the man who howled against the Treaty of Versailles.
Compared with Hitler, Clemenceau was tender toward Ger-

mans. So was Morgenthau with his plan for pastoralising Germany. The Fuehrer ordered that she be incinerated.

Thus we know at last that Hitler was a maniac even when dealing with his own people. Thus we know, as in a nightmare, the mind which would have been let loose on Europe had Britain followed France into defeat. And I see no reason for thinking that this maniac would not have had his war *quand même* even if the Allies had made none of the pre-war mistakes which A. J. P. Taylor and Liddell Hart attribute to them.

Speer and a few generals toured the country after Hitler gave his death-order, re-interpreting Hitler's commands and making them ambiguous. Within two months the Allies were giving their own orders for Germany. Speer seems to think he saved his country; but Professor Galbraith comments, 'This is nonsense'. Armies in total retreat cannot destroy everything they see, and in any case roads and rail lines and agriculture cannot be eradicated. With these and the minimum of shelter a nation can recover with startling speed. Industrial destruction is quickly repaired, as all the saboteurs in all the resistance movements found to their sorrow. And as Professor Galbraith points out, industrial capital is constantly being replaced so that before long the 'ruined' country has new instead of semi-obsolete equipment. This may seem like an argument for losing wars, and maybe it is if you are careful to lose to people like the British and the French and the Americans who only want to go home when they have beaten you and to be left in peace; but never lose a war to the Nazis, or to Genghis Khan.

I have quoted Churchill as saying, when Hitler offered 'peace', that the British 'now meant to have his blood or perish in the attempt'. This was an unusual declaration of ferocity, against an unusual enemy. Again and again, throughout the invasion summer, Churchill's sentiments were repeated by the Ministers of His Majesty's Government. *Nothing* would make them negotiate with Hitler or any member of his entourage or with any representative of a putative German resistance: noth-

ing, including the loss of their own lives and the lives of everyone they loved.

Wars are not usually fought on such terms. They are fought
for a definable end, such as land or money or the control of the
seas. The end is achieved, or denied, or stalemated. Then
peace may be argued; but who can argue with a man who
wished to enslave Europe and, when thwarted, wished to kill
Germany?

Civil wars, in the past, have been the saddest wars because
they are not negotiable without total defeat for somebody:
no longer a simple question of land or money, but 'Do I run
You, or do You run Me?' Hitler created a unique disaster, a
civil war within the whole western world: 'Do the Nazis and
their friends' (a famous American called them 'the wave of
the future') 'take over, or do we destroy them?'

Unhappily, a civil war hurts the victors almost as much as
the vanquished. Herbert Feis, historian of the diplomacy of
Hitler's war, writes: 'This is how the nature of the enemy influences not only the conduct of the war but what comes after.
The peace gets fitted to their faults and the fears they have
aroused. So the evil effect of men like Hitler and Mussolini
lives far longer than they.'

2

We have seen that on June 11, 1940, Churchill told the French
at Briare that if they felt they must capitulate 'let there be no
hesitation on our account'. This was most unusual and out of
character, for the decision to free the French from their promise not to make a separate peace was a matter for the War Cabinet, and Churchill was meticulous in consulting his colleagues.
However, on that sad June day he had just told Weygand
that there could be no more planes from England, no matter

what happened. His affection for France led him to be generous beyond his brief.

As late as June 15 the British Ambassador, Sir Ronald Campbell, was ordered to tell the French that in spite of the military situation the British refused to condone 'any action by way of negotiating with Hitler for a separate peace. M. Reynaud will be under no illusion as to what must be our attitude on this matter.' Defeat in the field was one thing and a cease-fire might become necessary. 'That is entirely different from the Government formally consenting to negotiate a peace or surrender. We have the example in Holland of the army surrendering while the Government yet survives and provides a rallying point for the national life of Holland and of her overseas Empire.' The French Government, if there still was one, should study the Dutch example and consider 'seeking asylum in the United Kingdom where we shall be most glad to receive them'. The all-important problem, Sir Ronald was reminded at the end of these instructions, was the French fleet.

On June 16 the British Cabinet relented and told Reynaud that he could go ahead and ask for Germany's terms provided, and only provided, that the French fleet was sailed to British harbours pending negotiations. On the same day Sir Ronald telegraphed that Reynaud was having his final confrontation with his colleagues. 'He would tell them that whatever might be the German terms or promises, France, if she failed her ally and made a dishonourable peace, would share sooner or later the fate of all countries which had fallen under the Nazis. Peace in such circumstances would mean centuries of servitude, and the reduction of France to the status of Slovakia. M. Reynaud would resign if he failed to get enough support.'

Reynaud did fail and did resign, to be succeeded by Pétain who cared nothing for France's promises to England. Pétain did not consult London; he simply asked the Germans to state their terms for an armistice. Thus died the last effort to entice the French fleet into British ports.

The French navy in 1940 was stronger than it had ever been,

even in the days of the American Revolution or in the days of
Napoleon when the French and Spanish fleets were briefly
combined. In 1940 the French had two great battle-cruisers
and the two most powerful battleships in the world. The latter
were launched and nearing completion. They could easily
have been commissioned in British yards.

Had such ships changed hands between the French and
English in 1940, countless lives would have been saved and
the winter of 1942–43 might not have been a nightmare to
the Allies. Had the ships fallen in 1940 to the Germans (who
had been too stupid to build themselves a proper navy before
going to war with Britain) the hinge of the world might have
changed. Since the days of the Armada all would-be conquerors of Europe had paused to ask 'What about the British
navy?' Now Britain was disarmed on land, threatened in the
air. If her navy were suddenly matched or over-matched
(for the Germans, too, had great ships building), the old question might be out of date.

In the armistice terms the French fleet was to sail to German or Italian ports. There the ships were to be disarmed
and the Germans promised not to use them during the war.

Could the Cabinet stake the life of England on such a promise, or on Admiral Darlan's promise to Churchill never to let
the French navy fall into German hands? The Nazi Government was staffed with liars who had been trained by experts
to remember that only the big lie convinces. Darlan hated
England and was jealous of the British navy.

Churchill and the War Cabinet had to attack yesterday's
friends, unprovoked, or jeopardise the future. The world was
to find that what Hitler called 'the brutality and tenacity of
its government', once war has begun, had not deserted
Britain.

General Ismay writes: 'The War Cabinet thought it would
be criminal folly to place any trust in Hitler's promise when
our very existence was at stake.' The same week Hitler said
to his intimates: 'With regard to the French fleet . . . the best

thing would be to have the French sink it. The worst thing would be to have the fleet unite with the British. In view of the large number of light French ships, the united British-French fleets could organise extensive convoys.'

Germany's disposal of the French fleet—or the leaving of so much of the French fleet for the British to destroy—remains a mystery. Above all else Hitler should have wanted it. He should have prepared a brutal descent on it, such as he prepared for the strongest fort in Europe, Eban Emael, which he took in a few hours with paratroops landing on the roof. While the French were dithering in Bordeaux, on the day Pétain succeeded Reynaud, he could have picked this priceless guerdon while no one was in a position to complain. Failing this, he should later have tempted the French to sink the fleet by pretending he was about to seize it and use it in spite of the armistice. Failing this, he should have bought Darlan (as the Americans did in 1942) or put intolerable pressure on the Government to hand over their ships. (Pétain chose to be at Hitler's mercy. Why should Hitler be merciful?)

He was not merciful; he was a land-mammal. He should have known in advance that England was the ultimate enemy (as so many conquerors had found before him) and therefore that the French fleet was worth more to him than all the slave-workers and all the doomed Jews and all the treasures that he stole from France. Hitler was not ready to steal the French fleet, so it was left to Churchill and his War Cabinet to make the horrid decision to attack it.

There is a famous book, in the world of geology and paleontology, called *The Land Mammals of Patagonia*. These mammals had a bad time: a sullen climate and an unfruitful soil. Being land mammals they could not escape. To the north it was too hot; in every other direction it was salt water. So they stayed at home for some millions of years and died with a minimum of complaint. Nature has treated the Germans far better. Weather is not fierce and natural resources are not denied. Yet the land mammals of Germany have been troublesome. For three generations they have made war. Unlike their distant relatives in Patagonia they could go to sea. And they did try, but always too late and too little. Land mammals they were in their blood. They should not have challenged sea mammals unless they could beat them in the third dimension of the air. This they thought they could do, and this they could not. So again, and for the last time, seamanship triumphed. The future belongs to the men of science, and thus to facts and machinery rather than to the poetry of the sea. Facts are supposed to be changeless. The sea is never the same, and it will never win another major war.

When it was decided to take or destroy the dangerous fleet, the French ships in British ports gave little trouble except for a scuffle over the submarine *Surcouf*. The French ships in Alexandria were controlled by Admiral Cunningham, who had superior forces and was a friend of the French Admiral Godefroy: a friend, but never an Ally. Godefroy was implacably anti-British to the end.

The French fleet in Algiers, at Mers-el-Kabir, was the danger. Here lay the great battle-cruisers. Admiral Somerville at Gibraltar had strength enough to sink or capture the Frenchmen. He was told to offer these terms: join the British and fight the war together; sail to a British port and be interned; sail to a French port in the West Indies and be demobilised, the crews being repatriated to France. 'If you refuse these fair offers, I must . . . require you to sink your ships within six hours. Finally, failing the above, I have orders . . . to use whatever force may be necessary to prevent your ships from falling into German or Italian hands.'

Admiral Sir James Somerville hated these orders and tried to protest. 'There was nothing for it', wrote General Ismay, 'but to give him a peremptory order to carry out the repugnant task without further question.' Churchill did his best to soften the 'peremptory order'. On the night before the day of the deed he sent a signal to Somerville: 'You are charged with one of the most disagreeable and difficult tasks that a British Admiral has ever been faced with, but we have complete confidence in you and rely on you to carry it out relentlessly.' So on July 3 the job was done. *Strasbourg*, one of the battle-cruisers, escaped with wounds to Toulon. The British command of the sea was secure. The Vichy Government broke off relations but did not declare war. Hitler was (or should have been) robbed of his last hope that the British would ever come to terms with him. On July 16 he gave his directive for the invasion of England 'if necessary'. He should have said 'if possible', for the invasion could not happen unless Fighter Command were destroyed. This the Fuehrer did not seem to understand. As early as July 6 he told Ciano[3] he was ready to 'unleash a storm of fire and steel on the British'. One day Germany would learn what such a storm meant. Meanwhile the British went about their business.

3

General 'Hap' Arnold of the American Air Force described the Battle of Britain in one sentence: 'On August 8 the R.A.F. Fighter Command took off to save everything, and between then and the end of September they saved it.' Nobody could improve on that. I shall only make a few comments and repeat a few figures and then discuss one of the strangest events of the war: the dismissal or downgrading, as soon as the world-preserving battle was won, of the Chief of Fighter Command and his right-hand man. They had saved our lives but not, it seems, in the way the Air Ministry would have chosen.

The 'domestic aspect' of the R.A.F.'s war, as Peter Townsend calls it, was a new form of heartbreak. Men used to go to war far-off, leaving their wives or mistresses to wait and hope: the regiments from Massachusetts at Gettysburg; the American Marines 'from the halls of Montezuma' to the South Pacific;

[3] Count Ciano, Mussolini's Foreign Minister and son-in-law.

the British in South Africa, France, the Crimea or the North-West Frontier; the French in Canada, India, South-East Asia, or too often in their own country; but even when fighting or dying in France the French soldier did not often see his home. The young men who won the Battle of Britain came home every night unless they were dead or burned beyond recognition.

'One left one's hotel in the morning', writes Townsend, 'to go out and die. If death was not at the rendezvous, one went back to the hotel for a drink with the boys'—or back to the cottage for a drink with the girl. Between leaving in the morning and returning (or not returning) when the day's work was done, there might have been two, three, four sorties. This was a rare strain on the women.

Townsend dramatised this 'domestic aspect' of the war with one story: 'Back in the mess at Digby the party had already begun as the last few pilots were still coming in to land. They entered the ante-room by ones and twos until there were two nineteen-year-old wives without husbands. Those girls knew they need not wait any longer . . . They just slid out of the ante-room. There was no fuss, no tears. They just left . . . They could have wrecked the morale of the squadron, but they never did.'

Defeat in a lost cause seems romantic: Roland, Marshal Ney, Robert E. Lee, not to mention endless Irish heroes who have become immortal for their failures. Victory in a 'lost cause' seems less memorable. If there was ever a 'lost cause' it was the Battle of Britain; but today instead of celebrating, the young men ask, 'If that was so glorious, why does the world still stink?' Had the cause really been lost, no such sharp questions would be permissible. Dictators are unaccustomed to being chivvied.

The hairy children who sit and scream in Grosvenor Square and throw stones at the American Embassy, or their cousins who march and scream on Pennsylvania Avenue and throw stones at the White House, would be purged at the first stone in the world from which the R.A.F. saved us. Yet the Hairy Ones should have a hearing, and in any case they are part of the future, and if we start suppressing the future we may be left with a rigid past, such as a 1,000-year Reich. The chance to disagree noisily and to throw stones was preserved by the Battle of Britain.

For stories of the death of criticism in a Nazi world, everyone should read Richard Grunberger's *A Social History of the Third Reich*. For example, a playwright called Rehberg got a poor review in the *Wuppertaler Zeitung*. The local party boss wrote to the paper's proprietor: 'The saddest and bitterest aspect of the situation is the fact that Rehberg has been a party comrade since 1930 (Membership No. 360,000). Perhaps your critic is not even a party member, or maybe a very young one, without any inkling of the depths of National Socialist culture. I am no longer prepared to tolerate sabotage by such malcontents at Wuppertal. At the very next opportunity I shall denounce these characters to Minister Goebbels and Minister-President Goering and shall demand that they be sent to a concentration camp.'

Then came the whip: 'As for yourself, I must ask you most cordially, as an old party fighter, to remove this critic at once.'

I have had some nasty reviews of my own plays but I should have been unhappy to see Charles Morgan (the writer of the nastiest) sent to a concentration camp or to hear that the editor of *The Times* was 'most cordially' ordered to sack his critic. We in the West should never make the mistake, or allow our children or grandchildren to make the mistake, of thinking that the Nazis were normal or acceptable. As for the 'good Germans' who accepted them, or repudiated them only by pretending they did not exist, one would have to be superhuman to pass judgment, or else live until late in the twenty-first century and have time to think things over. Today, I only talk about people who dared to call themselves Nazis. Such people were more numerous in 1941 than in 1945.

Another example of 'the depths of National Socialist cul-

1. The four representatives of the great powers who drafted the Versailles Peace Treaty. Left to right: Signor Orlando of Italy, Lloyd George of England, Clemenceau of France, and President Wilson of the United States.

2. The Munich Conference, September 29, 1938. Left to right: British Prime Minister Neville Chamberlain, French Premier Édouard Daladier, Hitler and Italian dictator Benito Mussolini.

3. Chamberlain waves scrap of paper—"no more war" pact which he signed with Hitler at conclusion of Munich Four-Power conference—as he arrives at Heston Airdrome, December, 1938.

4. Premier Benito Mussolini and Adolf Hitler shown during their historic meeting in Munich, July, 1940.

5. Charles A. Lindbergh and his wife, Anne Morrow Lindbergh, visit the home of Air Marshal Hermann Goering, right, during an inspection tour of Germany in 1936. Goering later presented him with the Service Cross of the German Eagle, one of the most prized German decorations, in 1938.

6. American observers of the war on British Isles. Left to right: Captain Kirk, U.S. Naval Attaché; Major General D. C. Emmons; United States Ambassador Kennedy; Brigadier-General Strong; Rear-Admiral Robert Lee Ghormley; Colonel Lee, Military Attaché, pictured in front of the British House of Commons, after they listened to Churchill's speech. This was the address to the British people rendering an account of Britain's war and in which Churchill revealed that an agreement "in principle" had been reached with the United States for the lease to it, as potential air and naval bases, of British possessions in the Atlantic from Newfoundland to the Caribbean, in exchange for the transfer to Britain of fifty over-age American destroyers.

7. General Maurice Gamelin leaving No. 10 Downing Street after attending the first meeting of the Inter-Allied Supreme War Council to take place since Paul Reynaud became French Prime Minister. March 28, 1940.

8. Dr. Joseph Goebbels.

9. Pierre Laval meets Hitler on Hitler's special train 22, October, 1940, during Hitler's trip to Frace, Spain and Italy.

10. Premier Paul Reynaud of France at his best and saddest is shown addressing the French Senate on the occasion when he announced that France was determined to fight the war to a finish until Hitlerism was crushed. He announced that the German Navy had lost half of its naval forces since the start of the war, most of these losses being inflicted since the German invasion of Norway. December 30, 1940.

11. German troops marching into Paris.

12. At Montluçon, Marshal Pétain leaves the town hall and passes under an arch formed by his comrades.

13. London air raid shelter at the Elephant and Castle underground station, November 11, 1940.

14. London, January 14, 1941. A "dry bath" is enjoyed by one of England's Pioneer Corps as he relaxes while off duty in the huge dump used to store materials salvaged from bombed buildings.

15. Willkie for his country. Wendell L. Willkie makes himself comfortable as he stresses a point while testifying for the lend-lease bill before the Senate Foreign Relations Committee on February 11, 1941. Willkie declared that the United States would be at war in thirty days should Great Britain collapse.

16. Colorado Springs, Colorado. Russell Davenport (left), who left the editorship of a prominent magazine to guide the presidential nomination destinies of Wendell Willkie and who helped Willkie make the destroyer deal, shown conferring with Willkie.

17. Hendaye, French-Spanish frontier. A German guard of honor presents arms as Chancellor Adolf Hitler (left) and Spanish Premier Francisco Franco pass in review.

18. General Maxime Weygand, who commanded the Allied Armies until the collapse of France, shown chatting with French war veterans somewhere in North Africa.

19. Oran, Algeria. The French battleship *Bretagne* is shown where it was beached during the historic battle of Oran in early July, 1940. The British opened fire after the French naval commander, Admiral Marcel-Bruno Gensoul, refused to accede to their demand to surrender. The British, who scored a decisive victory, took the action to prevent the units of the French fleet at Oran from being used by Germany against Britain.

20. General Archibald P. Wavell, Commander-in-Chief, Middle East.

21. Ernest Bevin at a conference of the Labour Party, London, July, 1941.

22. Herbert Agar (left) chats with Lord Greene in London, August, 1941.

23. The dome of St. Paul's Cathedral during the height of one of London's severest blitzes. Buildings around it were shattered with the dome wreathed in the smoke of their destruction and illuminated by the glare of the blazes. January 23, 1941.

ture' from which the Battle of Britain extricated us: Julius
Streicher, the top Jew-baiter for the Master Race, sent the following message to the readers who did not renew their sub-
scriptions to one of his papers: 'Your intention expresses a very
peculiar attitude towards our paper, which is an official organ
of the National Socialist German Workers' Party and we hope
you realise this. Our paper certainly deserves the support of
every German. We shall continue to forward copies of it to
you, and hope that you will not want to expose yourself to un-
fortunate consequences in the case of cancellation.'

These plans to corrode men's souls and self-respect shock
me more than the Nazis' pleasure in destroying men's bodies
inch by tortured inch. Doubtless I would have tried to save
my body at the cost of my soul, hence the shock. In any case,
those of us who survived the Nazi plague, once a dark shadow
from Berlin round the world, East or West, should give thanks
for what the men in Fighter Command—the dead, the maimed,
and the triumphant few—bought us. Dowding called them all
his 'chicks'. He mourned his lost chicks daily and deeply.

We, who have never been threatened with quick death or
slow death because of an opinion, forget how lucky we are to
be allowed to write even a book like this, which seeks to dis-
able a number of sacred cows. Nobody has told me what not
to say, and even better nobody has told me what I must say
if I am to stay out of prison, or out of an insane-asylum,
or out of the grave. In America it has become hazardous to
abuse the police or to throw stones in the wrong direction.
This is bad. Even so, a broken arm or a false arrest-and-
conviction is better than the ovens at Auschwitz. The Battle
of Britain gave America time to join the war, and later to consider her own salvation. Whether or not she chooses to save
her soul is a domestic problem; but the chance to save
her body, rather than have it trampled by Gauleiters, was
given by the boys who lounged in deck-chairs during that
magic summer of 1940, reading the *Daily Mirror*, waiting for

their second or third command since breakfast to go aloft and have another look at death.

As General Ismay explained to me a year later, with the help of hindsight and his long military experience, there was never a question of 'invasion' after the gamble which Inspector-General Milch urged upon Goering had been rejected. Thereafter the alternatives were victory for Britain in the air or the occupation of Britain by land forces. So long as Fighter Command prevailed, the land mammals of Central Europe could not invade. If Fighter Command were destroyed, invasion would be a waste of time. Occupation would be simple, quick and permanent. 'It would be a case', wrote Ismay years later, 'of "Movement Tables" and "Occupation Instructions" instead of "Operation Orders".' Then the sleepy giant in North America would find himself trapped between the Atlantic and the Pacific Ocean, both of which were owned by enemies.

> *Now comes the sick hour that his surfeit made*
> *Now shall he try his friends that flatter'd him.*

The 'friends' were the Nazis and their American Allies who preached that Hitler had nothing but kind thoughts about the United States and wished only to do abundant business with Chicago.

No one could know during that fateful summer that what General Ismay said a year later was correct. Yet the British remained illogically confident that even if Fighter Command were destroyed they could give the Germans some nasty shocks.

In the first place the armed forces (or the forces without arms) in southern England would not be hampered by refugees. That lesson had been learned by the B.E.F. in France. The men and women of Kent and Sussex are stern people. Forewarned, they could not be scared by any Stuka with a noise machine into blocking even a public footway. The War

Office, through the Ministry of Information, spread multitudinous pamphlets telling the public 'STAY WHERE YOU ARE'.

'If this island is invaded by sea or air', said one of these warnings, 'everyone who is not under orders must stay where he or she is. This is not simply advice: it is an order from the Government, and you must obey it just as soldiers obey their orders.

'WHY MUST I STAY PUT? Because in France, Holland and Belgium, the Germans were helped by the people who took flight before them . . . The soldiers who could have defended them could not get at the enemy.'

And so on, through many paragraphs of good advice ending: 'STAY PUT'! It's easy to say. When the time comes it may be hard to do. But you have got to do it; and in doing it you will be fighting Britain's battle as bravely as a soldier.'

Anyone who has lived among the British people will know that if they think staying put will annoy the enemy, 'put' is where they will stay.

Even more disconcerting to the Germans might have been the discovery that after they had crossed that vexing Channel with 'X' troops and 'X' tanks and transports they were in a land which had a flourishing 'Underground' and a 'Resistance' before there was anybody to resist or to go underground against. At this type of surprise the British lead the world. They subsequently taught most of Europe the tricks they had practised without any Germans to practise on,[4] also the horrid little weapons, easily concealed, which they were inventing for the reception of the invader.

David Lampe has told the story of the civilian 'stay-behind' troops who were recruited soon after the retreat from Dunkirk. General Thorne had been directed to prepare defences for the 'invasion coast' from Greenwich to Hampshire. He had few troops and less armour; but he was not too discouraged because he had been Military Attaché in Berlin and knew Hitler's ignorance of the sea. That land mammal thought the

4 Cf. Henri Michel, *La Guerre de l'Ombre*.

Channel was a wide river, instead of a trap for any fool who did not treat it with caution and respect. So the general thought in terms of sudden lethal raids, supported from the air, rather than of great armies pouring into Kent and Sussex.

He also remembered, Mr Lampe tells us, a visit he had paid to an estate in East Prussia. In the midst of peace, the peasants were building military defences on the hill-tops and stocking them with arms and food. His host explained that the land had been given by Frederick the Great on the condition that the owners should forever maintain a private army to attack invaders from the rear. They were not supposed to resist an invasion but to interfere with supply and support after the enemy's vanguard had passed by.

Since Britain had twenty-seven unarmed divisions to defend the entire country, and was searching her museums to find old weapons which might be more useful than beer bottles, General Thorne thought the East Prussian system might have merit in Kent and Sussex. The Home Guard (also unarmed) which had been called into being on May 14, was training to repel invasion from the air. Thorne's dream-guerillas were to harass a land-invasion from the rear. He asked General Ismay to send him an officer to train this wild, unlikely group and by good luck he was allotted young Peter Fleming of the Guards, probably the best man in England for the job. Widely experienced, totally daring, accustomed to doing things his own way, Captain (later Colonel) Fleming was the right man at the right time.

This odd new force was called 'Auxiliary Units' because the name means nothing. Aside from officers, it was recruited from people who knew their stretch of country intimately, from poachers to Masters of the local Hunt. Mr Lampe gives us many photographs of them and they are a cross-section of the English and Scottish countryside; village and farm. Their cover story was that they were members of the Home Guard with some special duties at night. They were ordered to tell nothing to anybody: a mistake, because as usual total security was merely a form of insecurity. Many wives thought that 'special duties at night' meant duties to mistresses and they soon found out, in their rural communities, what the words really meant. People who are trusted, in a small group such as an English village, are much more 'secure' than people whose curiosity is aroused and unsatisfied.

Many of the women who did find out what was happening were incensed because they too, in case of an invasion, were not given the chance to be killed almost at once. With no encouragement from the authorities they had organised an 'Amazon' Home Guard. They could not organise an Amazon 'Auxiliary Unit' since the units were not supposed to exist.

'An advancing army is not normally bothered by guerillas,' writes Colonel Fleming. 'They may involve an army of occupation in a costly diversion of effort, and they may be a source of real danger to a retreating army.' Modern warfare in 1940 (outmoded today) was an overwhelming horror. The victorious tanks and motorised artillery clattered through farms and villages whose residents were terrified and who either fled to become the prey of dive-bombers or cowered in their cellars for the pleasure of the Services of Supply who killed the men *en passant* and raped the women. Such was the fate of northern France; but England chose to be less passive.

The first plan for the Auxiliary Units was that they should all die quickly. Emerging from their hiding places they should interfere with Supply as much as possible before they were killed. They must either be killed or kill themselves, since they would know of other hiding places which might be revealed under torture. This was soon seen to be a wasteful plan, which might please rather than annoy the German invader. So the first experimental 'unit' (this sounds like Peter Fleming himself) invented a Chinese general of the fifth century B.C. who wisely said: 'A guerilla without a base is no better than a desperate straggler.'

Impressed by this Asiatic wisdom, Authority gave the unit permission to build large underground hideouts and to stock them with food, stoves, wireless sets and sabotage equipment. The latter grew more deadly each week. The unit was to operate about thirty miles inland from the bridgehead and a little more than thirty miles short of the first German objective.

Colonel Fleming compares these 'lairs' to the Lost Boys' subterranean home in the second act of *Peter Pan*. He does not seem to think that the Auxiliary Units would have done much damage had the Germans invaded. Yet Churchill was interested and thought the units should 'prove a useful addition to the regular forces'. And the Units were given submachine guns, .45 automatics, sticky bombs and a wealth of horrible little plastic explosive devices before the conventional British forces.

The first units were organised along the obvious invasion coast from Margate southwest to Bognor Regis. They were trained on the text-books of Major Colin Gubbins, later Major-General Sir Colin. (He was known as *Gubbski* in Poland where he went with Carton de Wiart in August, 1939, to teach his own strange form of warfare. He deserved such a charming, crazy name.) Gubbski's books of instruction were: *Partisan Leader's Handbook*, *The Art of Guerilla Warfare* and *How to Use High Explosives*. These deadly little pamphlets became the guides for most of the free world's resistance movements throughout Hitler's war. In England the Germans would not have been pleased to find Europe's best-instructed small-scale killers in their rear, just as they were recovering from seasickness.

The Authorities clearly believed in the Auxiliary Units because before long they were organised, in their Lost Boys' hideouts, from Pembrokeshire south, east and north the whole way round the coast to Dumfriesshire. The training was rigorous. Anthony Quayle, an Auxiliary Units Intelligence Officer in Northumberland for almost a year, tells how he learned to move through the night as noiselessly and as inconspicuously as one of Fenimore Cooper's Indians.

Later in the war, graduates from the units bec
in ambushing and killing Germans in unexpecte
Lampe gives many details.

Finally, on November 18, 1944, the Command
Home Forces decreed that 'the Operational Branch ᵥᵣ Auxiliary Units shall stand down. The time has come to put an end
to an organisation which could have been of inestimable value
to this country in the event of invasion.

'All ranks . . . are aware of the secret nature of their duties.
For that reason it has not been possible for them to receive
publicity, nor will it be possible even now. I should like all
members of the Auxiliary Units to regard it as a matter of special pride.' They doubtless did, being shy, brave villagers and
countrymen; but why the secrecy? Later, they all received an
extra piece of official nonsense: 'In view of the fact that your
lives depended on secrecy no public recognition will be possible. But those in the most responsible positions at General
Headquarters, Home Forces, know what was done, and what
would have been done if you had been called upon. They
know it well. It will not be forgotten.'

These reassuring voices are now stilled in death, so it would
have been forgotten had not Colonel Fleming briefly and Mr
Lampe in detail told us this lost story. And why lost? Because
of the inane desire of people in power to believe that they hold
secrets too precious for the rest of us to know. These men
were disbanded silently, without honours, more than five
months after D-Day and just before the Battle of the Bulge
after which German resistance in the West was a lost cause.
So who was keeping information from whom? The British
bureaucrats from the British people. The good story would
have made men walk prouder at the time. Today it's a tired
footnote to a forgotten blaze of patriotism. If that seems too
big a statement, remember that after an invasion all these men,
no matter how well they did their tricky jobs, were sure to be
dead before long. They were trained to kill and to explode
and to frustrate as long as possible; but in the end, their end,

they would still be on the spot, frustrating and exploding, hoping for a quick bullet and shivering at the thought of the Gestapo.

4

Returning to the 'lost cause' that was not lost, only a few figures are needed to dramatise the splendid summary by General Arnold. When the battle began in August, Dowding had about 528 fighter planes to guard England. Fighter Command was divided into groups. 11 Group, under Air Vice-Marshal Keith Park, covered the dangerous area from Portsmouth to the Thames estuary with twenty-one squadrons. Westward from Portsmouth was number 10 Group with seven squadrons. On Park's left (the east coast as far as Yorkshire) was number 12 Group under Air Vice-Marshal Leigh-Mallory with eleven squadrons. Number 13 Group defended the northeast and the north with ten squadrons.

On August 8, *Adlertag*, the first day of the fortnight during which Goering promised to destroy the R.A.F., the Germans had about 2,100 aircraft 'serviceable' and about 400 in reserve: 1,100 bombers, 700 Me.109 single-seater fighters and almost 200 two-seater long-range fighters. Roughly, it was 500 British fighter planes against 2,000 Germans, some 900 of which were fighters and the rest bombers whose job it was to take out the British radar masts and the British control stations.

The Germans knew more than we thought about British radar. They even had an inferior model of their own which they were busily perfecting. They were startled, however, to find that the British fighter pilot in the air was being told from the ground exactly where to find and kill his prey. Such accuracy made the old, slow Stuka dive-bombers (which had terrorised France and Belgium) useless. They were soon withdrawn. Their inventor killed himself, not because of his Stukas but because he was the first to see that Goering was ruining the Luftwaffe.

Among other Germans to be alarmed by Goering (and by British technology) was Adolf Galland, a superb fighter pilot. 'From the very beginning', he wrote, 'the British had an extraordinary advantage which we could never overcome throughout the entire war: radar and fighter control . . . The British fighter was guided all the way from take-off to his correct position for attack on the German formations . . . Our planes were already detected over the Pas de Calais while they were still assembling and were never allowed to escape the radar eye. Each of our movements was projected almost faultlessly on the screens of the British Fighter Control centres.' His briefings, he complained, would be three hours old by the time he reached the white cliffs of England. His British enemy's briefing would be a few seconds old.

Galland also complains that his High Command never decided which of three ways to use the Luftwaffe, so it used them in all three ways and never got anywhere. The first strategic decision might have been total blockade—to starve the island with the help of U-boats; the second might have been 'Sea Lion' (the invasion) which meant the destruction of Fighter Command; the third might have been demoralisation of civilians by night-blitz (Douhet's prescription). Goering tried them all but never persevered. As we all now know, the attacks on the radar masts were called off just as they were doing deadly harm. The attacks on the ground (or underground) stations which told the British pilots exactly where to attack their enemies were called off just as they were doing deadly harm. Later, during the night-blitz Goering never let his flyers finish a single job: neither the East End of London, nor Liverpool nor Bristol nor Plymouth. Even Coventry was back at work within a few days. (Galland says Coventry [November 14] was 'an accidental success'.)

The last day of the Great Blitz on London was May 10, 1941. A little later I had the fun of dining with the Chief of Air

Staff, Air Chief-Marshal Sir Charles Portal (later Marshal of the Royal Air Force Lord Portal). May, 1941, was not the high tide of British hopes, with neither Russia nor America in the war and everything going wrong in Greece and the Middle East. No one knew that the seemingly incessant blitz on London had ended. We only knew that on May 10 the Luftwaffe had hit the House of Commons, Westminster Abbey and the British Museum: a fair cross-section of British life and history.

Portal surprised me by saying, 'When we have won, the first man we should decorate is Goering. He has dispersed and half-ruined the Luftwaffe—far more than we could have done so quickly.'

'Peter' Portal, as his friends called him, looked younger than his years: dangerous and charming. He enjoyed falconry, and looked like a thoughtful hawk who had been educated at Winchester. I felt myself lucky to be a friend and not an enemy of this perilous man. I wondered whether the people of England shared half his confidence. A few days later I went to El Vino in Fleet Street, where in the early thirties I used to exchange with other journalists what we hoped was information. The barman, friendly as of old but a little wary of me as a neutral, said I could not buy bottles of wine, though I could have as much as I could hold, standing at the bar. 'You see, Sir, I have to keep my cellar as full as possible for my steady customers after the war.' So it was not just the hawk-like Portal who assumed that the war must be won somehow, somewhere.

The Nazis boasted and shouted about their coming victory. The British took victory for granted without raising their voices. As Harold Nicolson wrote in his *Diary* on February 14, 1941, at the height of the blitz: 'Yet through all this regret and dread pierces a slim clean note of pride. "London can take it." I believe that what will win us this war is the immense central dynamo of British pride. The Germans have only assertiveness

to put against it. That is transitory. Our pride is permanent,
obscure and dark. It has the nature of infinity.'

5

No matter how brave and victorious men may be, they usually manage to blot or to confuse the fair record with their
own imperfections. Behind the glory of the Battle of Britain
lies a tangle of broken promises and of strange accusations in
high places. I cannot unravel the tale but I can describe it, and
since I knew the hero and the semi-victim of the whole mish-
mash I can have the pleasure of praising him.

In July, 1936, Hugh Dowding was made the first
Commander-in-Chief of Fighter Command when the Air Defence of Great Britain ('a ponderous system', as Dowding
called it) was divided into Bomber, Coastal and Fighter Commands.

Ever since 1931, when the British had won the Schneider
Cup for the third time at 340 m.p.h., Dowding had been
pressing to use this Rolls-Royce Merlin engine and some of
the Schneider Cup sea-plane's design for a land-based eight-
gun fighter. Hence, in the end, the Hurricane and the Spitfire.
Also, like most of the professionals, the 'fighter-boys' who had
survived the first war, he saw at once the all-importance of
radar. He was the first to begin devising the use of land-to-air
directions. Yet someone on high, for hitherto unknown reasons, kept harassing this necessary man. He was told he was
to be made Chief of the Air Staff. Then he was told, abruptly,
that he was not. He did not mind the decisions; but he did
object, mildly, to the rudeness.

As the Battle of Britain approached, Dowding and his organisation and his 'chicks' were the only hope. He was still
being pestered by orders to resign, orders which were with-

drawn as soon as they were issued, like a swarm of demented insects infecting his headquarters.

Dowding was the calmest man I have known. I wonder whether anyone else could have taken this inspired discourtesy in his stride. And I wonder whether anyone else could have prepared his 'chicks' to face death with the feeling that at least they would not die through someone's folly.

Air Vice-Marshal Keith Park was Dowding's right-hand man as Senior Air Staff Officer at Fighter Command. As we have seen, Park was put in charge of the all-important 11 Group for the Battle of Britain, covering the whole of the area most vulnerable to German attack. Park's twenty-one squadrons consisted of 250 single-seater fighters. Dowding was criticised on high for giving so many planes to 13 Group (ten squadrons defending the northeast and north)—until the Germans attacked from the north with abundant bombers but too few fighters, thinking the north would be easy meat. The attack was totally destroyed and one criticism was silenced.

Churchill's comment was: 'The foresight of Air Marshal Dowding in his direction of Fighter Command deserves high praise, but even more remarkable had been the restraint and the exact measurement of formidable stresses which had reserved a fighter force in the north through all these long weeks of mortal conflict in the south. We must regard the generalship here shown as an example of genius in the art of war.' These lines were not written by a man who would permit plots against Dowding. The plots came from belowstairs.

When 11 Group was exhausted and with no reserve, Park would call on 10 Group to his right and help came fast from South African Air Vice-Marshal Quintin Brand. It did not come, or did not come in time, from Air Vice-Marshal Leigh-Mallory on Park's left (where the eleven squadrons of 12 Group defended the east coast). Leigh-Mallory was not a 'fighter boy' from the first war, like the rest of them. He had been an Army Co-operation flyer. Perhaps he was jealous; he was certainly ambitious and stubborn. He and Park had crossed swords while Park was Air Staff Officer. Leigh-Mallory now criticised, loudly and among politicians, the Dowding–Park plan to meet the Germans with single squadrons which could be airborne in minutes. Leigh-Mallory said the defence should depend on wings of three to five squadrons. These took much longer to assemble after the radar said the Germans were on their way. When Park noted that this might be the reason why 12 Group never came to the rescue on time, the horrid little war-within-a-war began.

Strangely (or not-so-strangely to anyone who has watched politics for a lifetime), the fact that Dowding and Park were right made no difference. Leigh-Mallory disobeyed his orders and produced his Big Wing too late for most occasions. Park and Dowding won the Battle of Britain. Or maybe Goering won it for them; but at least the British did not lose it. Leigh-Mallory usually did nothing decisive, except verbally.

September 15 was 'the culminating date' for Goering. He could no longer pretend to master Fighter Command. On September 19 the invasion operation 'Sea Lion' was postponed indefinitely. In October, Dowding was replaced as Head of Fighter Command by Sholto Douglas. Park was replaced by Leigh-Mallory and sent to Training Command. Before these changes, Dowding and Park were called to a meeting at the Air Ministry. They must have assumed that they were called for congratulations. Instead they were cross-questioned as to why they had not used Leigh-Mallory's Big Wing theory. Nobody seems to have remembered that they had saved the West.

This can have nothing to do with air warfare. It smells of politics. The great men were busy on the world stage, so the little men in the ministries were serving their friends or their grudges. Three things, I think, are clear. First, Churchill had nothing to do with this. In spite of Wavell's warning that Dowding's days were numbered because he had no more fighters for France, the great Churchill knew all about man's debt to Park and Dowding. He had been present at 11 Group on a day when every squadron was engaged and there was no reserve and the map table showed waves of new Germans crossing the coast. Park's 11 Group survived, diminished, as night came. General Ismay drove back to Chequers with the Prime Minister, whose first words were, 'Don't speak to me; I have never been so moved.' Five minutes later he said as if to himself, 'Never in the field of human conflict has so much been owed by so many to so few.'

Second, it is clear from letters that A. J. P. Taylor has found in the Beaverbrook Library that the Secretary of State for Air, Sir Archibald Sinclair, a courtly man, was never rude or disregardful of Dowding's feelings. The bad manners came from below.

Third, Beaverbrook was in favour of Dowding and would have made more trouble for Dowding's enemies had he not been so busy fighting his own enemies in the Services, from whom he was stealing materials to build more Spitfires.

My own footnote is simple. Dowding and I had a common friend and after all the fuss was over I used to lunch with them whenever possible. I shall never understand how Dowding got the nick-name 'Stuffy'. He was shy; but he was a charming, warm companion. By the time I knew him, perhaps discouraged by this alarming planet, he had become interested in spooks. Discovering politely that I did not share this interest he never mentioned the matter again. He did not care to talk about the Battle of Britain; but even with his two main interests excluded he was a man of such wide culture that he gave pleasure by his presence. And he never complained of what had been done to him.

Park was less other-worldly. 'To my dying day,' he said, 'I shall feel bitter at the base intrigue which was used to remove Dowding and myself as soon as we had won the Battle of Britain.'

As for Leigh-Mallory, his end sounds like one of Belloc's *Cautionary Tales*. I have mentioned that he was stubborn. When, later, he was posted to the Far East, he set out for Gibraltar in a storm rejecting the advice of the weather experts and of his own pilot. The Pyrenees proved more stubborn than Leigh-Mallory.

6

On September 4 Hitler made an hysterical speech at the *Sportpalast,* ending with a clear promise to invade England. 'When people are very curious in Great Britain', he said, 'and ask *"Yes, but why doesn't he come?"* we reply *"Calm yourselves! Calm yourselves! He is coming! He is coming!"'* Then he got excited, even for Hitler. 'When they declare that they will increase their attacks on our cities,' he yelled, 'then we will raze their cities to the ground . . . When the British air force drops three or four thousand kilograms of bombs, then we will in one night drop 200,000, 300,000 or 400,000 kilograms.'

Three days later he did the opposite of 'coming': he began the bombing of London, thus saving Fighter Command, which neither he nor Goering had the sense to feel was close to collapse. September 15 was Park's last day of agony, with all his squadrons in the air, and all the squadrons he could borrow and not a plane in reserve had the Germans made one more push; but they did not.

On October 7 Goering defined the aims of the blitz: 'Progressive and complete annihilation of London', paralysing Britain's war potential and civil life, and 'the demoralisation of the civil population of London and its provinces'. Goering was as misinformed as the Committee of Imperial Defence had been when predicting the results of indiscriminate bombing. (It was night-bombing Goering was describing, so it had to be indiscriminate.) By the time he made these bloodcurdling statements he was in the position of King Lear:

> *I will do such things,—*
> *What they are yet I know not—but they shall be*
> *The terrors of the earth.*

King Lear could not; and neither could Goering, who had lost his air war against England by the time his blitz began. Fighter Command had been on the edge of defeat when the bombing was turned from their precious 'sector stations' on to the East End of London. A month later Fighter Command had more pilots and machines than when the Battle of Britain started. And the two-seater night fighters were proliferating. This is not to suggest that the blitz was agreeable, but merely that it was useless.

One of the reasons it was useless was Lord Beaverbrook, Churchill's Minister of Aircraft Production since May 14. Beaverbrook's appointment did not please Churchill's new Secretary of State for Air, Sir Archibald Sinclair. No one could tell where Sinclair's powers began or Beaverbrook's ended— no one except Beaverbrook who assumed that in a division of powers he had the lion's share.

Two generations of men and women have argued fruitlessly about this astounding man who was a major figure in both the German wars, helping to unseat Asquith in the first and to sustain the Royal Air Force in the second.

The R.A.F., when the whirlwind called Beaverbrook took over, needed sustaining. Chamberlain's Government had devised a gentle programme of rearmament which might have given Britain her maximum military strength by the end of 1942. Beaverbrook saw at once, on May 14, that he did not have two years and might not have two months to produce the airplanes to save our world. Ignorant or contemptuous of Civil Service rules, accustomed to playing both Tsar and Rasputin in his own little Empire, he built a new, confusing Ministry overnight. He was distasteful to the people who knew the 'rules' and thought them sacred and to the people who played politics down the middle of the road, uncommitted. Even in his cradle Beaverbrook must have taken sides violently, a noisy and contumacious infant.

He knew that fighters, and in a few months night fighters, were all that stood between Britain and slavery. So the 'rules' went overboard and with the silent help of the Prime Minister he stole much of the stuff which the army and the navy craved. He made enemies wholesale. Civil Service departments are even more deplorable than normal men and women once jealousy is aroused. 'The Great Disorganiser' Beaverbrook was called; but the planes were there, in barely sufficient numbers, for the Battle of Britain and the blitz. 'Barely' is the word. The Ministry of Aircraft Production was not in full swing, ready to start its miracles, until early August. Goering, in the same week, thought he was set to erase Fighter Command. Then the production surged forward. In six weeks there were more fighters, for day and for night, than before the Battle for France.

Beaverbrook's contribution to victory has been half-forgotten because of his showmanship. This was easy for his enemies to deride and is still easy to remember. His 'pots and pans for victory' produced masses of useless aluminium; the park and garden railings which he commandeered diminished London's beauty but were no good for munitions: the 'Spitfire Fund' raised many millions of pounds which gratified the Treasury but built no Spitfires. You cannot build Spitfires with money. Men and goods were in short supply, not sterling. Yet the people who surrendered their saucepans and their sterling and who lamented their park railings felt that they were a tiny bit more involved in the majestic struggle. Even the showmanship, which looks tawdry today, may have been worthy in 1940.

Nobody of my generation, nobody who watched Lord Beaverbrook in action for more than fifty years, and certainly nobody who is emotionally committed for or against, can make a wise judgment about this enigmatic man. The young may have forgotten him; but the young of the future, if they study history, will not forget him. For this was a man, with all the usual human faults and failures hugely exaggerated. This was also a Power, who made history and did not merely suffer it. The only writer so far who seems to know Beaverbrook affectionately and dispassionately is David Farrer, the title of whose 'personal memoir' stirs old memories: *G-for God Almighty*. Love him or hate him, it's the right title.

So London was not annihilated by Goering and the civil life of Britain was not demoralised. The new war, the war of the night fighters which Churchill named the 'wizard war', turned to England's advantage in a few months because the British wizards were better than the German ones. Later I shall tell of the social and political changes brought by the blitz. Here, although bomb-stories have become an international byword for boredom, I shall give one such tale. I take it from the Croom-Johnson diaries. It epitomises the worst fears of blackout-plus-bombing, short of mutilation or death. If it happened to me, I think I should have died of fright.

In February, 1941, a friend of Croom-Johnson was driving home to Hampstead at midnight. Suddenly the blackness became total, as if he had gone blind. Even the faint lights of the other motor cars disappeared. He stopped and tried to get out. He felt himself enveloped in a soft oil-and-silk substance like an opaque, slimy spider's web. When he struggled free he found that he and his windshield were caught in a parachute. Clear of this blinding web, the first thing he saw in the faint night-light was a land-mine sliding smoothly off a low roof on to the ground. The mine and its parachute had got entangled with a chimney.

These huge mines were supposed to land on a pair of horns which detonated them. This one landed on its nose, horns in the air, else there would have been nothing left, large enough to identify, of car or driver or house. The blast would throw a man, or bits of him, a quarter of a mile.

Thus the blitz, for the survivors. In October Croom-Johnson lamented: 'Only two theatres open: the Windmill with its long bare legs and the Vaudeville with "All's Well that Ends Well".' And on New Year's Eve he summed up the year 1940: 'The prospect is considerably brighter than anyone would have dared to hope at the beginning of July. Unless we get knocked out in early spring . . . I don't see the war ending in 1941.'

This was not what Goering had planned. On October 20 he had stopped all day-time bombing of England and the night fighters took over. At first it did not seem silly to think that the abundant German terror-bombers might demoralise a small island. Within three months it was clear that they could not.

The decisive failure of the Luftwaffe was partly owing to the British wizards and partly to Goering. The fear and pain, the homelessness and the deaths caused by the blitz, were at their worst in the East End of London where the housing was ramshackle and the over-crowding endemic. Had Goering persisted, for months on end, in pounding and burning and terrorising only the poor and badly housed, he might have created a feeling of 'two nations' even among the English, even in London with its resilient and humorous Cockneys. The Cockneys knew that the old (and in war-time useless) who had money had mostly escaped west or north to a safe hotel or to a safe country house. They also knew that professional men and women who had money, if they were not killed or mutilated, would never be inconvenienced by the blitz as they themselves were inconvenienced: witness Croom-Johnson, a solicitor, whose office was blown up and whose flat was burned out. He found friends with whom to live and other friends to lend him office-space. And if he felt he was imposing on his hosts, he could always live at his club.

Luckily the Cockneys also knew that the young of all classes had gone to war, not with the ignorant joy of 1914, but with the sombre knowledge that the British Isles were at stake and might be taken and enslaved. This made for unity, no matter how diverse the sacrifice.

Nevertheless, had Goering waged a strictly 'class war' against the poor in London and Glasgow and Liverpool, and against the miners of South Wales, sparing the privileged and the lucky ones everywhere, he might have divided the British people. This was worth trying. Instead, he united his enemies by attacking the poor, the rich, the half-rich and the Royal Family indiscriminately. The bombing of Buckingham Palace was equivalent to the loss of a Panzer Division on the battlefield. Goebbels saw this, too late. He broadcast that the Luftwaffe was aiming at huge oil-storage reservoirs cunningly concealed in the neighbourhood of the Palace.[5]

7

The first problem which was presented to the British wizards, in order to diminish the horrors of the blitz, was to adapt radar to the needs of a plane flying through darkness and cloud. During the daylight Battle of Britain a plane could be directed from the ground to within easy sight of its enemy; but at night all was bewilderment. The pilot could be told that a German plane was in his vicinity; but he would usually lose it unless he ran into it.

'Night after night we chased around after rumours and found nothing', complained C. F. Rawnsley, the air gunner (later the navigator) for the famous John Cunningham. The searchlights from below were sometimes helpful, but not often. They could not shine through 10,000 feet of cloud.

The first attempts to use radar inside the night fighters seemed hopeless. Yet when a civilian Scientific Officer (a 'Boffin' to the boys in the R.A.F.) explained the principle, it sounded simple enough. 'You shout "Boo" across a valley', said the Boffin, 'and after a while the echo shouts "Boo" back at you. You time the interval, and knowing the speed of sound you can work out the distance across the valley . . . Now if

[5] A Mr C. Paley Scott wrote a letter to *The Times* suggesting that since the oil tanks at Buckingham Palace had been destroyed, the submarine base at Berchtesgaden deserved attention. (Dated September 15, published September 18, 1940.)

you use some sort of directional ear trumpet, like a sound lo-
cator, you can spot your "Boo" exactly.'

The 'Boos', or 'blips', worked splendidly so far as the distance from the target was concerned. The directional ear-
trumpet, without which the distance was a useless statistic,
remained a problem for months. Little by little the Boffins improved their ear-trumpets. Air gunners like Rawnsley became
navigators—not by sight or by stars but by their magic boxes.
The tale, with its fierce discouragements and occasional break-
throughs, is told dramatically in the Rawnsley-Wright book.
The figures explain the frustration, since by the end of the
major blitz they were still negligible compared to daylight
fighting. They were enough, however, to discourage anything
but sporadic raids once the Germans turned their bombers
against Russia.

In January, 1941, the Germans lost only three planes to the
night fighters, and in February only four. Then in March
they lost twenty-two, in April forty-eight and ninety-six in
May. The night fighters, navigated by radar, had become a
serious enemy to the bomber, as the British discovered two
years later when they began their massive raids over Nazi Europe. The German wizards had caught up.

The faith which the pilot of a night fighter had to place in
his navigator was absolute. Rawnsley says it was like 'driving
a very fast car, with no lights and no brakes, on a dark night
down a winding unlit road close behind another equally fast
car with no lights. Let the driver then shut his eyes and keep
them shut, and let him rely entirely on his passenger's instructions to keep him out of trouble.' The navigator 'was in the
position of the passenger, breathlessly trying to keep the blind
driver on the road'. The pilot had to obey these wild instructions exactly: impossible, but he had to do his best. If the
navigator ever got close enough to see the other plane (with
eyes, not radar) the pilot would do the shooting and then veer
off to escape the débris.

The first Heinkel which the Cunningham–Rawnsley team

a clear night. Rawnsley watched it all the way
ground. He felt sick when he saw the splatter.
Cunningham. 'That'll teach them to crack nuts
ie harsh remark was to calm his navigator's nerves.
gham was the gentlest of men but the deadliest
of enemies in the night skies. He was annoyed at being called
'cat's eyes' because he knew that his night-sight was normal.
He also knew the Germans must be kept from guessing the
secret of his successes. The second legend, that he could see
in the dark because he ate carrots, did not bother him and
presumably did not fool the Germans; but it got a lot of people
in blacked-out England eating a lot of carrots, one of the foods
which were in ample supply at the time.

8

In spite of the terrors and the suffering and the many thousand
dead, the blitz was as big a Nazi failure as the attack on
Fighter Command. The British people were brought closer
and not divided, made stronger and not frightened. Nowhere,
except briefly in places like Coventry and Bristol and the East
End of London, had life been dangerously disorganised—and
the important word is 'briefly'. There were no plagues and no
epidemics, both of which the Germans had expected.
Strangely, the health of the stubborn islanders improved.
Dodging bombs makes the adrenalin flow. Fire-watching and
digging neighbours (whole or in parts) out of rubble gives a
sense of purpose which may be lacking in peace-time. And as
we shall see in a later chapter, the blitz and its counterpart the
evacuation paved the way for many hopeful changes in the
British way of life.

The blitz, the 'Great Blitz' on London, ended on May 10,
1941. Hitler was glad to turn from the irritating little island
toward the vast plains of Russia. He had little to boast about

in his war on England. The British army escaped at Dunkirk. Fighter Command escaped and 'saved everything'. The blitz misfired and the invasion never took place. The last failure was the sum of all the others and drove the Wehrmacht eastward toward cold despair. The uninvaded island stood ready to support great armies when they gathered to prepare the end of the Third Reich.

V
Meanwhile in the
United States . . .

1

In 1934 the American Embassies in Tokyo and Berlin were warning Washington that the Japanese and the Germans had ambitions for expansion which seemed unlimited. Unlimited ambitions mean war, since peace is a balance of ambitions which is just tolerable to the Great Powers. (Peace could also be a world cured of nationalism; or it could be a desert.)

Franklin Roosevelt doubtless listened to these early warnings; but neither the public nor the Congress did. As we have seen, in 1935 Congress passed the Neutrality Act which imposed an arms embargo on both sides in case of war. The Act was extended the following year, and again in 1937 with the proviso that oil, scrap iron, rubber and cotton might be sold to belligerent nations who could pay cash and who would carry the goods in their own ships. This last was a tiny step forward since in Churchill's words it rendered 'to superior sea power its full deserts'.

The folly of the Act, or of any attempt to legislate a nation into neutrality in the midst of a world-wide civil war, was shown when Japan attacked China in 1937. The Act would prevent China (then a favourite of the American people but lacking factories) from having arms to save herself from Japan (an unfavourite, but highly industrialised). Also Japan, under cash-and-carry, could buy anything she chose in the United States whereas China, lacking a merchant marine, could not. The only way out of the ludicrous trap was to pretend that since Japan had not declared war nothing at all was taking place. So the President never invoked the Neutrality Act. Officially there were no belligerents. The country approved although a few Senators growled and grumbled.

In spite of this sharp lesson from Asia, the Foreign Relations Committee of the Senate refused, in July 1939, to discuss changes in the Neutrality Act during that session. The President then called together a group of leading Senators from both parties. He and the Secretary of State urged them, almost begged them, to change their minds, assuring them that the world was on the edge of disaster and that the United States would be useless and helpless if she could not even sell arms to her friends while refusing aid to her enemies. It was at this meeting that Senator Borah of Idaho, archisolationist, told Cordell Hull that he (the Senator) had his own sources of information 'and on several occasions I found them more reliable than the State Department'. Hull was not a patient man but he managed to keep silent. Six weeks later Germany invaded Poland.

Like most interesting comments made in confidence at the White House, Borah's untimely boast was Washington's gossip the next day. When war came at once, the Senator's arrogance did not help his cause, or rather it did help the Administration since Hull clearly knew what he was talking about and the Senator did not. In the future the isolationists would not defeat Roosevelt face-to-face; but they would cause him to drag his feet drearily.

On September 8, when the war was a week old, President Roosevelt told a press conference: 'There is no thought in any shape, manner or form, of putting the nation, either in its defences or in its internal economy, on a war basis. That is one thing we want to avoid. We are going to keep the nation on a

peace basis, in accordance with peace-time authorisations.' In
a statement to the nation he seemed less complacent: 'I hope
the United States will keep out of this war. I believe that it
will. And I give you assurance and reassurance that every
effort of your Government will be directed toward that end.'

Robert Sherwood (who knew the President well and served
him devotedly and assessed him with a detached wisdom)
comments: 'This may be denounced as, at worst, deliberately
misleading, or, at best, wishful thinking. The inescapable fact
is that this is what Roosevelt felt compelled to say in order to
maintain any influence over public opinion and over Congressional Action.'

Sherwood is right. A week later F.D.R. called the Congress
into extraordinary session to modify the Neutrality Law. He
had hoped for an outright repeal but his friends in Congress
told him this was impossible. The arms embargo could only
be lifted if cash-and-carry were substituted and if loans to belligerents were forbidden and if American ships were excluded
from combat zones. This was pusillanimous but possible: a
long step forward from the total rebuff in July. The President
accepted.[1]

I watched the debate in September 1939 from the Press
gallery of the Senate. One might have thought the President
had asked permission to sell the United States to England.
The Opposition was hysterical and seemed wholly devoted
to keeping the United States out of the war. The same with
the mothers and children who stormed the corridors of the
Senate building, screaming about 'Merchants of Death', 'the
House of Morgan', 'British Propaganda' and similar phrases

---

[1] A month before Pearl Harbor the entire Act was at last repealed
by a narrow vote in the Senate and in the House of Representatives.
Meanwhile the absurdity of the Act had been underlined. When Germany invaded Russia the Neutrality Law was not invoked, so that the
harbour at Vladivostok might stay open for American shipping. Just
as when Japan invaded China, nothing had happened—except that this
time the two most ferocious armies on earth were clawing each other to
death.

from long ago—not a pretty picture of democracy at work in
the making of foreign policy. In the end the President got his
half-way. He had to declare that this cash-and-carry compromise, which would have embarrassed Shylock, was the clearest
road to 'American peace'. At this time I believe Roosevelt
thought (as did most of us) that France and Britain could win
in the West and there might be such a thing as peace in the
United States. Cordell Hull agreed. 'The President and I,' he
wrote, 'long before the outbreak of war, saw clearly that it
would be to our own national interest to assist Britain and
France, first in the effort to keep the war from coming, and
second, to win the war if it came. We knew that a German
victory over Britain and France would place us in direct con-
tact with the ruthless leaders of Germany riding a powerful
military machine. With Japan on a rampage in the Orient, our
position would be of the utmost danger.'

This is reassuring as to foresight; but Hull adds, 'With isolationism still powerful and militant in the United States, it
would have been the peak of folly to make aid to the democracies an issue in connection with neutrality legislation.' He
may well have been right; but it seems a pity that the peak of
folly would have been to tell the truth. Hull and the President
were vastly experienced. They knew better than anyone else
what could and what could not be done. They decided to
change the Neutrality Act—to abolish it if possible—without admitting that this was 'aid to the democracies'. They assumed
that an uproar would have been the price of truth-telling. The
assumption raises questions about the durability of democracy.

Cordell Hull, before becoming Secretary of State, had spent
a long life in Congress, praised for his wisdom but disregarded
when it came to action. 'I was listened to but not heeded,' he
wrote. 'My Congressional experiences as a Cassandra in the
Twenties were being transplanted to the foreign field in the
Thirties . . . I had warned again and again that with economic nationalism trade would fail, debts could not be paid,

unemployment would ensue, and collapse would surely come. It came . . . From the State Department . . . I warned even oftener that, with political and economic nationalism, war would surely come.'

It came. And Cordell Hull did not dare warn his people that by sticking to a rigid 'political and economic nationalism' they were not evading war but prolonging the inevitable pain. Perhaps nobody could have spoken usefully during the weeks when Poland was being overwhelmed.

When France, also, was shattered the picture changed for many of us, including the President. Sherwood writes: 'At this point I am sure he (F.D.R.) became convinced—and this is not speculation—that if Britain fell disastrous war for the United States would be inevitable, that Germany would attack the Western Hemisphere . . . and that Japan would concurrently go on the rampage in the Pacific.' So the fall of France, a torment to so many millions of people, presented the President with an unexpected challenge. He enjoyed challenges; he saw that Britain must not fall. What could he do to help? The American people were bent on avoiding 1917, not on facing 1940. If the President said what he thought, he would lose control of his deluded public. If he said what he didn't think, the facts would soon expose him and he would be accused of double-dealing. If he said nothing he would betray the greatness of his office. In the end he did a little of all three: occasionally daring, occasionally prevaricating, occasionally sphinxlike.

2

In 1917 (the year most of the isolationists seemed still to inhabit) Roosevelt was Assistant-Secretary of the Navy in Woodrow Wilson's Cabinet. He watched the tergiversations of that unhappy President who had proclaimed himself ignorant of foreign affairs just before foreign affairs became the only thing that mattered. Early in 1916 Wilson had sent Colonel House to Europe. France seemed on her last legs and the President knew enough to see that France must be supported; but House went too far in trying to make Prime Minister Briand happy. House reported to Wilson that 'it was finally understood that . . . you would intervene' unless the war took a sharp turn for the better. This may have been Briand's understanding. It was not Wilson's. The war took a sharp turn for the worse, but this was an election year in America. Wilson won his election in November by a tiny margin on the slogan, 'He kept us out of war'. A few months later the United States was at war 'to make the world safe for democracy'. The excuse was absurd since democracy cannot be made safe.

Wilson had started foolishly in August, 1914, by urging the American people to be neutral in thought as well as in deed. Such a plea could only make sense if America's national interest was not involved. If Wilson had educated his public from the beginning in simple geo-politics he need not have presented the war, when America entered, in language so emotional and moralistic that it returned to haunt him. Most Americans thought they were fighting to improve mankind rather than to save themselves from the disaster of German victory; so they were disillusioned when mankind remained sullenly unimproved.

Wilson had no excuse for walking into this trap. His closest friend and adviser, Colonel House, had written him on August 22, 1914, that if Germany should win 'we will have to abandon the path which you are blazing as a standard for future generations . . . and build up a military machine of vast proportions.' And the Colonel said in his diary that Wilson agreed. In July, 1915, he wrote again to the President: 'I feel we are taking a terrible gamble ourselves in permitting our safety to rest almost wholly upon the success of the Allies.' Two months later Wilson told House that 'he had never been sure that we ought not to take part in the conflict and, if it seemed evident that Germany and her militaristic ideas were to win, the obligation upon us was greater than ever.'

Such views had been familiar to students of foreign affairs ever since the 1890s, when men like Henry Adams and John Hay began saying that America's safety depended on an Atlantic community strong enough to keep Germany from dominating France and England. Wilson knew American history. So why 'neutral in thought'? And why the subsequent nonsense about being 'too proud to fight'? In any case he got himself into an unholy tangle, and he could only get out of it by presenting the war, in 1917, as some sort of a belated crusade.

Wars are not idealistic. They may be selfish and relatively harmless, like the wars of the eighteenth century. They may be life-and-death and totally harmful like the wars of the twentieth century. Wilson tried to make his necessary war more popular by hitching it to the American belief in progress, a belief which he himself shared. He truly thought that the world would get better and better as time passed, as if this were a law of nature. He was a pure Gladstonian liberal. A terrible event like war needed a tremendous excuse. Preventing German victory was not good enough, so it became the war to end wars. And when it did nothing of the sort it became the war to promote cynicism and isolationism, the war which 'proved' that America must never again get herself entangled with Europe.

Thus Wilson, having misnamed his war and misinformed his people, lost his peace, his part in the League of Nations, his health and his credibility. Repudiated by the public, he became the excuse for every American avoidance of world responsibility.

None of this was lost on Wilson's Assistant-Secretary of the Navy, who was to become the most adroit of American politicians and who was to be faced with a Germany even more harmful than Wilson's and who promised himself that he would never lead the country into war until the country knew it was in total danger.

Franklin Roosevelt may have seen, as early as the fall of France, that America was in such danger; but the people saw nothing of the sort and were not too pleased to be told it (as we war-mongers quickly learned). Cordell Hull wrote that he and the President knew that aid to Britain was essential for the good of the United States; but the people at first found no reason for giving a fig to Great Britain. So here was a pretty dilemma. Roosevelt would not lead the country into an idealistic war because he had watched what had happened to the last man who did so. He believed that the present war was a life-or-death affair; but the public was so far from agreeing that he would have lost all influence had he said what he believed. He was confident that if Britain fell the Americas, North and South, would be in grave (perhaps mortal) danger. Most people disagreed; but most people wanted Britain to win so long as they themselves were not inconvenienced. So this was one point on which the President might hope to get the people behind him. Aiding the British became the undignified but inevitable foreign policy of the Administration. And assuming that Britain could prevent invasion, the place where she most needed aid was at sea.

3

The loss of merchant ships, during the twilight war, was not frightening: 200,000 tons in the first six months, compared to the loss of 400,000 tons in one month in the spring of 1917. In 1940, the loss which might be deadly to the British was the loss of destroyers. From the moment the battle of France began on May 10 (and ended militarily, so far as the Continent of Europe was concerned, before June 1) the fleet had to prepare for rescue at Dunkirk and for invasion. Many of the destroyers, the all-duty ships which are expendable when disaster threatens, could not be spared for convoy duty. Forty-one destroyers were used to lift 100,000 men from Dunkirk. Six of these ships were sunk and twenty-six badly damaged.

From the outbreak of war to the end of 1941, the Germans claim to have sunk by U-boats 2,432 ships (8,938,828 tons). By bombing and by mines they claim another 388 ships (1,002,424 tons). Before the end of 1943 the Allies were building more ships than the Germans could sink and sinking more U-boats than the Germans could build. In May of 1943, for example, the Germans lost forty-one U-boats, which was nearly double what they built. Radar and air power had won the Battle of the Atlantic: a battle as important for the British Isles as the Armada, and far more important than Waterloo.

In the course of the whole war the Germans produced almost 1,000 U-boats; of which 779 were sunk and fourteen captured or lost in storms. Had those 700, or half of them, existed in the autumn of 1939, Great Britain would have been starved by the time France accepted the armistice. Vice-Admiral Sir Arthur Hezlet,[2] British Submarine Commander 1941–45, says that if Doenitz had been given 300 U-boats at the outbreak of war he could have sunk the whole British merchant fleet in nine months. This would have been a few days after the French armistice; but presumably Britain would have surrendered long before.

'There are seldom less than 2,000 British merchant ships at sea,' wrote Winston Churchill, 'and the sailings in and out of our home ports amounted each week to several hundreds of ocean-going vessels and several thousands of coastwise traders.' The losses of April, 1917, had been diminished by the new system of convoys. In September, 1939, convoys were introduced when war began; but convoys mean destroyers and the Royal Navy was short of destroyers.

Captain (later Admiral) Kirk, the U.S. naval attaché in London, explained to Washington on June 12, 1940: 'In home waters, the situation is growing desperate . . . The need for destroyers to combat invasion, for anti-submarine work, and

[2] Foreword to H. A. Werner's book.

for the support of armies on the French coast precludes any reinforcement for the Mediterranean Fleet. In September, 1939, the Royal Navy had 153 effective destroyers in commission but now have about 100 . . . as compared with the total of Allied destroyer strength of 530, at the time of the armistice of 1918 . . . New destroyers are needed at once.'

On May 15 Churchill made his first plea to Roosevelt for the gift, or loan, of American destroyers. (This was the day Churchill was woken by Reynaud who insisted that France was lost.) The Prime Minister knew that after the First World War the United States had put in moth balls more than 150 destroyers; not as fast as these ships should be, hard to handle, no defences against aircraft, but still destroyers. He also knew that in September, 1939, sixty-eight of these ancient vessels had been reconditioned to serve on what was called a 'neutrality patrol' off the coast of North America. (Someone must have thought them worth something.) Churchill may or may not have known that Admiral Stark (Chief of Naval Operations), when asking Congress for money to revive these ghosts, had testified that they were needed for the defence of the United States.

The Prime Minister got a dusty answer from the President; but the request for destroyers led to one of the most interesting arguments in war-time American politics. The British finally got the fifty destroyers (in September). Whether they were too late, or too useless or too expensive, or whether they saved the day, depends upon which British Admiral you read.

Admiral of the Fleet Lord Tovey said: 'I thought they were the worst destroyers I had ever seen, poor seaboats with appalling armament and accommodation.' On the other hand, Admiral of the Fleet Sir James Somerville wrote: 'Had there been no American "four stackers" available, and had they not gone into service escorting trade convoys when they did, the outcome of the struggle against the U-boats and the subsequent outcome of the European war itself might have been vastly different . . . They served us well.' And Admiral of the

Fleet Sir George Creasy, Director of Anti-Submarine Warfare in the Admiralty at the time, writes: 'Admittedly many of them were an appalling headache to keep running. But, taken by and large, they gave invaluable service at a time of really desperate need.'[3]

4

Certainly we who were fighting the political battle for the transfer of the destroyers thought the situation desperate and the ships useful. Our case at first seemed hopeless. The more we stressed the dangers to America, should Britain fall, the less sense there seemed in giving away part of the fleet. This was a contradiction inherent in the undignified plan of trying to save America by providing other people with weapons with which to die.

I think the most unattractive title ever devised was 'The Committee to Defend America by Aiding the Allies'. If our country needed defending why did we not defend her, instead of asking the French and the British to do the job? Unhappily, few citizens thought America needed anything except larger and more abundant motor cars. The President knew better; but the President was hamstrung by a complacent Congress, and the Congress was in tune with the majority of the people.

After the first startling German successes, the President could get all the money he wanted for defence, but not for offence. On May 16 (the day after Reynaud's despairing call to Churchill) Roosevelt asked Congress for $1,200 million and a plan for 50,000 airplanes. Two weeks later he asked for $1,300 million to build a new army and a two ocean navy. The money was quickly voted—and it was high time. The army

[3] The quotes from Admirals are all from Philip Goodhart's book on the destroyers. Cf. Bibliography.

had 200,000 troops with weapons mostly from the First World
War. The air force had acquired fifty-seven new combat planes
during the first three months of 1940. The navy slumbered at
Pearl Harbor.

The money was voted; but there was no rush to build the
ships, the planes, or the new army. 'Business as usual' prevailed. We who had asked for war on Germany, on June 10,
had foreseen that the United States would never rearm herself,
let alone give decisive support to Great Britain, without an
economic upheaval in which labour, capital and consumers all
agreed to sacrifice for the nation. This does not happen among
free people except in time of war or of some similarly hateful
catastrophe. We war-mongers knew that the enemy was at
the gate, that the threat to our life was immediate, and that
time was running out; but most of our fellow-citizens did not
agree. So all we could do in our frustration was to use our several influences, whenever the chance came, to push the country
towards war. The British plea for destroyers was such a
chance.

We now had a little war-mongering office in New York and
we met frequently at the Century Club to discuss who could
do what in the way of promoting an act of war against Germany. We took the view that we might run out of Englishmen
to fight for us. We had been joined by powerful friends since
the 'Summons to Speak Out'. We had influence among journalists, and among politicians who did not quite dare say what
they thought. (Our isolationist enemies dared, because they
had the majority behind them.) We also had knowledge of
the American scene, and sufficient access to the British Government and the British Embassy in Washington to know what
was wanted (in the way of goods rather than of talk) by the
only people who were fighting our war. Number One on the
list was 'the destroyer-deal'. The problems were mountainous;
but we were told the need was absolute.

On June 15 Churchill had sent the President another telegram: '. . . We are now faced with the imminent collapse of

French resistance and if this occurs the successful defence of this island will be the only hope of averting the collapse of civilisation as we define it.

'We must therefore ask as a matter of life or death to be reinforced with these destroyers. We will carry out the struggle whatever the odds but it may well be beyond our resources unless we receive every reinforcement and particularly do we need this reinforcement on the sea.'

At the same time the President was told by his Ambassador at the Court of St James's that the British had nothing left but their courage. Yet the President wanted, and intended, to send those destroyers. He also wanted, and intended, to be re-elected in the autumn for the first third-term Presidency in American history. Were the two 'wants' incompatible?

Admiral Stark, Chief of Naval Operations, had recently testified to Congress that these old destroyers should be refitted and re-commissioned for the defence of the United States. The President, by his silence, had agreed. And the Walsh[4] amendment to the Naval Expansion Act of June (1940) said that the Chief of Naval Operations must certify that any 'surplus' vessels (whether loaned, sold, given or scrapped) were 'not essential to the defence of the United States'.

If the President had asked the Congress to repeal the Walsh amendment, the Congress would have refused. Such was the trap. Perhaps no one but Franklin Roosevelt could have wriggled out of it. Four things he wanted: first, a national hero to tell the people that the transfer of the destroyers was in their own interest; second, a promise that Wendell Willkie (his Republican opponent in the election campaign) would not attack the 'destroyer-deal' (if it ever came off); third, a valid and popular excuse for by-passing Congress and simply doing the job as Commander-in-Chief of all the Armed Forces; and fourth, he also needed, though he would not have put it this way, a press and radio campaign stressing the fact that

[4] Senator Walsh was another Irishman from Boston who scorned the English.

since we were not willing to defend ourselves we must help the British to defend us. On three of these four fronts, the war-mongers could help. Yet the timetable was heartbreaking in its delays.

On August 1, three of us went to see the President, asking whether there wasn't something we could do to help him on the 'destroyer-deal'. He said, 'Yes.' He said he wanted General Pershing, on a nation-wide radio hook-up, to tell America that the 'destroyer-deal' was wise, and well considered, and neces-sary. He said he himself could not ask General Pershing, be-cause everything a President says leaks, and he would be accused of using a national hero to promote a cause which the Congress would not have approved.

'If one of you asks Pershing to make the speech,' said the President, 'it probably won't leak. If it does, and you say the idea came from me, I shall call you a liar and all would be peaceful in Congress.'[5]

I was chosen as the 'one'. I went to see the General in a hotel three blocks from the White House. I was afraid of failure. I had been the humblest member of the navy in the First World War and thus had never even seen the general. I need not have worried. His old friends had already been urg-ing him to speak out. He wanted to speak out. All he needed was a word from the President. This I was privileged to bring him, and he was pleased.

'I wrote to the President', he said, 'when Germany invaded Poland. I said that we Americans would be in a sad way if Germany conquered Europe. I said I knew nothing about politics, or of what was politically possible; but I believed that as his senior General I should tell him what I thought.'

Whether the President was honestly afraid of a leak if he telephoned from the White House to the General, or whether he sent me on this mission to keep me out of mischief, I shall never know. He wanted us war-mongers to feel that we were

[5] The quotation is not accurate. This is how I remember it after thirty years.

useful and that he was giving us good guidance. He did not want us to go off the handle and demand what could not yet be done for fear we should lose such influence as we had and thus lose all our usefulness to him. He could be most sharp—mostly through Robert Sherwood as his mouthpiece—when he thought we were being 'impractical'. As time passed, as the United States (without quite admitting it) became more and more involved in the world's great tangle, he used us more and abused us less. Used or abused, we were content because we felt we were doing all we could.

At the time of the destroyer-deal, the Third Term election was the most important event in the United States. We had to watch our step, since many of us were known to be known to the President, lest we contaminate him with our extreme views. These may well have been his views also; but he had to wait for time to prove him correct and so soften the hard hearts of the isolationists. Time did its job, but in an awkward fashion.

Having accepted eagerly the suggestion for a nation-wide broadcast, Pershing asked me whether Walter Lippman would help us in drafting the speech. I said I was confident he would; and he did. Joseph Alsop helped on the final draft. The speech was broadcast on August 4.

The General said, in part; 'No war was ever prevented by hiding the danger and by arguing the danger does not exist . . . More than half the world is ruled by men who despise the American idea and have sworn to destroy it . . . It is my duty to warn you, before it is too late, that the British navy needs destroyers and small craft to convoy merchant ships, to escort its warships, and hunt submarines, and to repel invasion.' He added that the United States had 'an immense reserve of destroyers' and that if we gave the British at least fifty we might help to save the British fleet and thus, as he explained in his peroration, we might even help to save the human race.

The General was not too happy in explaining that our role was to equip other people to fight our battles. He seemed to feel that we might fight them ourselves; but he had been told by his commander-in-chief that this speech was a necessary step, so he took it gallantly.

We did not know, when the three of us saw the President on August 1, that the destroyers were to be discussed at length the next day, at a meeting of the Cabinet where all agreed that the deed should be done but the majority thought it impossible. Roosevelt's own notes on the meeting said: 'It was the general opinion, without any dissenting voice, that the survival of the British Isles under German attack might very possibly depend on their getting these destroyers.

'It was agreed that legislation to accomplish this is necessary.

'It was agreed that such legislation, if asked for by me without any preliminaries, would meet with defeat or interminable delay in reaching a vote.'

Harold Ickes, the Secretary of the Interior, adds in his *Diary:* '. . . It was clear that there were two things we ought to ask for. First, that the British fleet be sent over here if Great Britain could not beat back the Germans, and second, that we be given the right to use Britain's naval bases on our Atlantic coast. . . . A joint use seemed to be acceptable to the President and to the Department of State.'

When it came to the disposal of fleets and naval bases, this was a matter of high policy between the heads of governments. Private citizens were not welcome; but on another front the President had dug his toes in and said that he would do nothing without a promise from Wendell Willkie not to make the destroyers a campaign issue. This was asking a lot because it would have been a good campaign issue had Roosevelt persisted in the face of a hostile Congress—which he might have done, because although supreme in judging the probabilities he was also supreme in stubbornness and did not care to be crossed when he knew he was right.

Willkie was a freshman in politics. He had been lifted, as if out of a magician's hat, only three months before the Republican nominating convention. Unknown young men weary of the perennial candidates, Dewey and Taft, had sprung to arms all across the Continent to support this agreeable warrior whom nobody knew and whom nobody, therefore, disliked. Important newspapers fell in line; funds were forthcoming. Luckily for us all, Willkie was somehow nominated. He was defeated; but he never tried to tell the American people that they could be safe cowering behind their diminishing oceans. He might have won by lying; but he was not a liar.

Since the manner (the speed) of his nomination was unique in American history, and since he did not even know the names of the thousands of state and county workers who would determine his fate throughout the Continent, Willkie was avid for 'issues'. He was soon being accused by leaders in his own party of being a 'me-too' candidate, who only differed with F.D.R. on small stuff such as the treatment of the private owners of Public Utilities. (No matter how attractive they may be at home, these are not vote-winning people.)

We war-mongers (now known as 'the Century Group') had two assets in asking for Willkie's help. First, Willkie was an honest man who would choose to be defeated rather than win on a false issue; second, we had among recent recruits two men to whom Willkie would listen and who could explain to him the importance of these outmoded little ships.

The first was Lewis Douglas (later Ambassador to the Court of St James's) whose gently-expressed wisdom kept many of us, many times, from harming our cause and who became an unofficial chairman at most of our meetings at the Century Club.

Mr Douglas persuaded us that on this issue (destroyers) we must work closely with 'The Committee to Defend America by Aiding the Allies'. The Committee was organised nation-wide, while we were not, as yet. The Committee was respectable because it never admitted where its policies led, whereas we were suspect because we always used the dread word 'war'. Thus the respectable and the outrageous joined hands on a programme of broadcasting and news-letters and advertisements to tell the public that the destroyer-deal would safeguard our shores.

Lewis Douglas, during these frightening days, was in the West and so was Willkie and they were in touch. We hoped hourly for the news that would unleash the President.

Our other recruit for this campaign was Russell Davenport, managing editor of *Fortune* and co-ordinator of the campaign to nominate Wendell Willkie. He was also one of Willkie's best friends. Thus we had better helpers in the Republican camp than the President could hope to mobilise.

Willkie, after the fight to win the nomination, was resting in Colorado Springs. Both Mr Douglas and Mr Davenport kept in touch with him and thought that any day he would speak the words for which the President waited. Suddenly Arthur Krock, head of the *New York Times* bureau in Washington, stated in his column that 'the high military command of the Navy Department opposes the transfer of these vessels'. He added that Willkie was being asked not to attack a transfer of the destroyers but that he, Arthur Krock, could see no reason why Willkie should tie his own hands.

Clearly impressed by this (and Arthur Krock was an impressive figure with long and intimate knowledge of the Washington scene) Willkie announced that a 'candidate for the President of the United States should reserve for himself an unhampered right of public discussion'. This seemed the end to all our hopes: yet Lewis Douglas and Russell Davenport persevered. They felt they must put the dreadful facts before the candidate and that he would make up his own mind, irrespective of Mr Krock's 'high military command'.

While waiting and hoping for the liberating word, Roosevelt and the Prime Minister were settling the question of naval bases and of a renewed promise about the British fleet. Churchill grumbled about the promise, since he had already made himself clear; but he said he would fit the statement in somewhere, some time. He did not grumble in the least about the bases. As he wrote in Volume Two of *The Second World War:*

'There was, of course, no comparison between the intrinsic value of these antiquated and inefficient craft and the immense permanent strategic security afforded to the United States by the enjoyment of the island bases . . . Believing, as I have always done, that the survival of Britain is bound up with the survival of the United States, it seemed to me and my colleagues that it was an actual advantage to have these bases in American hands.' He also reflected that the transfer of these warships, in the middle of a war, 'was a decidedly unneutral act by the United States. It would, according to all the standards of history, have justified the German Government in declaring war upon them. The President judged that there was no danger, and I felt there was no hope, of this simple solution of many difficulties.'

The heads of the two Governments differed on one point. Churchill wanted the whole thing to be an exchange of gifts, one gift unrelated to the other. 'It is the fact', he cabled to the President, 'that we had decided in Cabinet to offer you naval and air facilities off the Atlantic coast quite independently of destroyers or any other aid.' He added: 'I see difficulties, and even risks, in the exchange of letters now suggested or in admitting in any way that the munitions which you send to us are a payment for the facilities. Once this idea is accepted people will contrast on each side what is given and received. The money value of the armaments would be computed and set against the facilities, and some would think one thing about it and some another.'

This was a delicate way of putting it: '. . . some would think one thing about it and some another.' In fact, if the question of 'money value' was ever raised everyone would think the same thing: that the British had been grossly overcharged. Churchill, naturally, did not want to be criticised at home for making a bad bargain; but Roosevelt did want to be praised at home for making a selfish one. There was an election coming in less than three months and the President did not dare appear as merely generous and far-sighted. He wished to appear as a shrewd Yankee trader. Hence, in all the discussions, the lectures, the letters to the press, there was constant discussion of the *quid pro quo,* the wonderful benefits America was to receive for making a tiny gesture toward saving the world.

In the end the two great men agreed to compromise. Many of the bases would be presented as a free gift to America. A few would be in exchange for the destroyers. They also agreed to misunderstand each other a little and not to look too carefully into how the deed was interpreted on the other side of the Atlantic.[6]

On August 20 Churchill announced to the House of Commons 'amid great cheering' the decision to lease to the United States certain 'sites in our transatlantic possessions' to make easier the common defence of the Western Hemisphere. Nothing was said about destroyers. Nothing could be said about destroyers, because Washington was still waiting on the word from Willkie. So Churchill got his magnanimous gesture.

In New York, meanwhile, one of the most important letters ever written to a newspaper had solved Roosevelt's third problem; how to by-pass Congress and hand over the destroyers on his own authority as Commander-in-Chief of the Armed Forces.

Napoleon said that a written Constitution should be brief and obscure. The American Constitution is both. In times of great danger the powers of the Executive seem unlimited. In

[6] Some phrases abide in the mind through the years and can make one feel discouraged even after half a lifetime. *Quid pro quo* is such a phrase for me. I was travelling the country during these critical weeks, trying to persuade editors to support the 'deal' if it ever came to pass. They all asked, what was the *quid pro quo?* When I assured them it would be far more than we deserved, they all seemed happy rather than thoughtful. The question of winning the war was still thousands of miles away in their imaginations.

tranquil times (or in what the people feel to be tranquil times) these powers fade alarmingly. Such was Roosevelt's problem. He knew the times were dangerous beyond description; but a majority of the people did not agree. How far could he use his executive powers and still be re-elected?

President Jefferson once bought a third of the continental United States (excluding Alaska) for fifteen million dollars, a fair bargain. He admitted that he had no authority for such an act; but the country was in danger, the opportunity came to hand and since he was dealing with Napoleon it might be withdrawn at any moment. So he acted, unconstitutionally, and the people on the whole were delighted.

Remembering this, Dean Acheson and his friends set to work to show that in another time of troubles the President could act, perhaps not even unconstitutionally, to protect the country. Their conclusion was published on August 11, in a letter to the *New York Times*. The names attached could not have been more resplendent in the profession of the law, and the results of the letter could not have been more startling.

We have seen that the Cabinet and the President himself, who did not like being thwarted, felt that nothing could be done about the destroyers without legislation. Now came the fresh thought which changed everything. The arguments, which took three and a half columns of the *New York Times*, were complicated and somewhat strained; but the astonishing fact was that this legal brief convinced the President, the Attorney General, most of the Cabinet, and finally the Chief of Naval Operations himself, that they had all been wrong in thinking that new legislation was needed for the destroyer-deal. The Constitution, they now agreed, was more pliable than any of them had thought.

By the end of August the negotiations with Great Britain were completed. We were all waiting for the promise from Wendell Willkie, without which the President would not move. On August 30, in the evening, the good news came to the Century Group. Lewis Douglas and Russell Davenport had prevailed. Willkie promised his friends that he would not attack a transfer of destroyers.

On September 3 Roosevelt announced the destroyer-bases agreement to the nation. He used the precedent of Jefferson's Louisiana Purchase and implied that the whole thing was a shrewd horse-deal on his part. Churchill, to the House of Commons, implied that it was a simple matter of two good friends helping one another.

Officially, Britain 'gave' the United States a lease on bases in Newfoundland and Bermuda and the United States 'exchanged' fifty destroyers for a lease on bases in the Bahamas, Jamaica, Antigua, St Lucia, Trinidad, British Guiana.

More than three and a half months had passed since the first cry went out from London for this meagre help. The will to do the right thing was there, in the White House and among the Cabinet. The will was there among thousands of leading citizens; but the opposition was also there, scattered at large throughout the vast federal Republic. Yet at long last Roosevelt got his way. Dowding and his Fighter Command had bought the necessary time. When drafting his message to the legislature, Roosevelt said to his Secretary: 'Congress is going to raise hell about this, but even another day's delay may mean the end of civilisation.'

No wonder democracy is a hazardous way of life.

5

The destroyer-deal may or may not have been a small affair in the war; but it was a big affair in the United States because it wounded the Demon King 'Neutrality'. Lend-Lease, on March 11, 1941, saw the death of the Demon. Edwin S. Corwin, the historian of the American Constitution, called it 'a qualified declaration of war'. Sherwood called it 'a common law alliance'. Churchill called it 'the most unsordid act in the history of any nation'. A. J. P. Taylor, never to be caught agreeing with the majority, called it the ruin of Great Britain as an exporting power. Everyone believed it was the end of American neutrality. Yet the whole political fight for Lend-Lease was based on the statement that it was the one way of keeping the United States neutral. Even the three members of Roosevelt's Cabinet who had long wanted war had to be silent now that war was clearly on the doorstep.

Harold Ickes, the Secretary of the Interior, wrote in his diary on June 15, 1940 (the day after Paris was occupied), that he wanted the United States to declare war on Italy and Germany.[7] Frank Knox, about to become Secretary of the Navy, wrote to his wife, also on June 15: 'The sooner we declare war the sooner we will get ready.' Henry Stimson, the evening before he became Secretary of War (June 18, 1940), said on the radio that America should send all her military aid to Britain in American ships convoyed by the United States navy. This meant war. Yet they all kept quiet while the battle for Lend-Lease was fought on the pretence that here was a smart device to evade war.

I have been correctly quoted as writing at the time that the notion that Lend-Lease was meant to keep America at peace was 'bunk'. The purpose of the quotation was to suggest that by writing this I was criticising the President. Not at all. As a free journalist I could say what I thought. The President, half-enslaved by American superstitions about 1917, and responsible for the safety of the nation, could not enjoy the fun of expressing himself flatly. His job was to get the bill adopted and to get the war won as soon as possible. If this meant double-talk, so did most foreign relations in the midst of

[7] 'The old curmudgeon', as he was called by his friends and (in a different tone of voice) by his enemies, told me this at the time. He seemed jealous of our 'Summons to Speak Out', since this is probably the only time in his life when he did not speak out. He could not continue the job he was doing at home, for the American people, and oppose the Administration's 'no-war' policy.

a world revolution. Before exploring that statement, here are the main facts about Lend-Lease.[8]

On August 2, 1940, Ickes wrote a letter to the President in support of the destroyer-deal. He ended: 'It seems to me that we Americans are like the householder who refuses to lend or sell his fire extinguishers to help put out the fire in the house that is right next door although that house is all ablaze and the wind is blowing from that direction.'

A few days later, talking to William Bullitt, his ex-Ambassador to France, Roosevelt put the same idea and ended: 'How do you think the country and the Congress would react if I should put aid to the British in the form of lending them my garden hose?'

The President knew (although he hated to admit it) that British funds were about to run out. He thus knew that the days of 'cash-and-carry' were numbered. He knew that the fall of Britain would mean America at war under the worst possible circumstances. And he knew that the large majority in both Houses of Congress accepted none of these facts. So what to do?

In August, I don't think he had the slightest idea; but he had a happy confidence in himself and in his muddle-through. He also had a happy faculty for putting off decisions until the last possible moment. And he never worried. Perhaps these are the qualities Oliver Wendell Holmes had in mind when he said that Roosevelt had 'a second-class intelligence but a first-class temperament'.

In any case, he saw the problems as early as August and he didn't worry. In September he got his destroyer-deal and in November he won his election. On December 1 he gave permission for the British to place orders for ships far beyond their ability to pay. He spoke vaguely about financing these orders on 'the loan idea'. The next day he went off with Harry Hopkins on the cruiser *Tuscaloosa* for two weeks in the

[8] The details are all in Dr Warren F. Kimbell's book. Cf. Bibliography.

Caribbean, perhaps to look at the new American bases but probably to get away from Washington and have a little time to think.

Churchill's view of the British position, at the time of the President's relaxing cruise, was desperate. 'Up till November, 1940,' he wrote, 'we had paid for everything we had received. We had already sold $335,000,000 worth of American shares requisitioned for sterling from private owners in Britain. We had paid out over $4,500,000,000 in cash. We had only two thousand million left, the greater part in investments, many of which were not readily marketable. It was plain that we could no longer go on in this way. Even if we divested ourselves of all our gold and foreign assets, we could not pay for half we had ordered, and the extension of the war made it necessary for us to have ten times as much.'

Afflicted with this money-nightmare, Churchill began working on what he thought may have been the most important letter he ever wrote: a letter to the President on British finances. It is reprinted in full in *Their Finest Hour*. He worked on it for weeks. It was delivered to the President on board the *Tuscaloosa* on December 9.

Churchill writes: 'Harry Hopkins, then unknown to me, told me later that Mr Roosevelt read and re-read this letter as he sat alone in his deck-chair, and that for two days he did not seem to have reached any clear conclusion. He was plunged in intense thought, and brooded silently.'

He had plenty to brood about. The eleventh hour had come. Britain could not survive on her own financial resources. When it came to paying for the multifarious arms and ships she required if she were to go on fighting, she was broke. Until this moment Roosevelt had pretended to cling to the myth of Britain's inexhaustible resources. Now the United States must somehow pick up the bill or she would find herself lonely, bereft of the only people who were prepared to die so long as America handed them arms. Churchill did not put it

that way. He was most courteous; but life is not courteous.
You either pay the price or you go under. The closest Churchill
came to this bald statement was in paragraph seventeen of his
letter:

'. . . As you know, the orders already placed or under ne-
gotiation, including the expenditure settled or pending for
creating munitions factories in the United States, many times
exceed the total exchange resources remaining at the disposal
of Great Britain. The moment approaches when we shall no
longer be able to pay cash for shipping and other supplies.
While we shall do our utmost, and shrink from no proper
sacrifice to make payments across the Exchange, I believe you
will agree that it would be wrong in principle and mutually
disadvantageous in effect if at the height of this struggle Great
Britain were to be divested of all saleable assets, so that after
the victory was won with our blood, civilisation saved, and the
time granted for the United States to be fully armed against
all eventualities, we should stand stripped to the bone. Such
a course would not be in the moral or economic interests of
either of our countries.'

After another paragraph, the letter concludes: 'If, as I believe, you are convinced, Mr President, that the defeat of the
Nazi and Fascist tyranny is a matter of high consequence to
the people of the United States and to the Western Hemisphere, you will regard this letter not as an appeal for aid, but
as a statement of the minimum action necessary to achieve
our common purpose.'

'I didn't know for quite a while what he was thinking about,'
said Harry Hopkins of Roosevelt's brooding on the *Tuscaloosa*,
'but then—I began to get the idea that he was refuelling, the
way he so often does when he seems to be resting and care-
free. So I didn't ask him any questions. Then, one evening, he
suddenly came out with it—the whole programme. He didn't
seem to have any idea how it could be done legally. But there
wasn't a doubt in his mind that he'd find a way to do it.'

The President returned to Washington on December 16 and

the next day at a press conference he tried out his garden-hose analogy: 'I don't want fifteen dollars—I want my garden hose back after the fire is over.' He was asked what would happen if the hose were damaged. The borrower, he said, would later replace it. The purpose of his plan he said, was 'leaving out the dollar mark in the form of a dollar debt and substituting for it a gentleman's obligation to repay in kind'. This was so vague as to mean nothing: but the reporters, stupefied by the daring of the whole idea, did not press Roosevelt. They did ask who would have the title to the goods thus transferred to Britain. 'I don't know,' said the President, 'and I don't care.'

'Who was this Franklin Roosevelt?' asks James MacGregor Burns, his latest biographer. The question is exigent; but it will not be answered in my lifetime. Mr Burns suggests a few of the manifold Roosevelts: 'the master-campaigner . . . ; the son of Hyde Park . . . who had measured men and events by old-fashioned standards of *noblesse oblige;* the Democratic-coalition politician who had learned to barter and compromise with Tammany chiefs, union leaders, city bosses, Western agrarians, Republican moderates and isolationist Senators.'

He was all of these Roosevelts, and many more which Mr Burns lists. Some day historians may fit the whole lot into a single skin. Today I know nobody who even pretends to see him whole. We must all agree with Frances Perkins, his old friend and his Secretary of Labour: 'Many books will be written about Franklin Roosevelt but no two will give the same picture . . . He was the most complicated human being I ever knew.'

All I can add from my own fascinated but not bewitched experience is that he had Wilson's view of the powers of the presidency, Jefferson's stubbornness and taste for the politically devious, a zest for responsibility which recalls his fifth cousin, Theodore, and a complication of character behind which he could rest himself from the loud, demanding world. He was too much of a back-patter for my taste; but this came from welding Hyde Park with the toughness and resilience

to fight the ultimate corruption of the democratic city machines
—most of which he destroyed in the name of honest government. Had he survived he might have finished the job in Chicago. At home, he met the people's demand for action and for
the positive state. Abroad, out of his magician's top hat, he
produced Lend-Lease. He did not solve unemployment at
home and he did not go to war until he was compelled; but
he did better on both fronts than anybody else could have
done.

Yet in spite of his political sagacity and his worldliness,
Franklin Roosevelt was subject to sudden bouts of optimism
which have no place in modern life and which made him
sound at times almost as naïve, almost as nineteenth-century,
as Woodrow Wilson.

Early in January, 1941, before his third-term inaugural message, he appeared before Congress to tell the astonished legis-
lators about the Four Freedoms. This was a beautiful speech,
beautifully delivered, but about as true-to-life as the kindness
of Water Rat in *The Wind in the Willows*.

In the midst of the blitz on London and on the other major
towns of England, with the Italians invading Greece and Hitler about to send Rommel to maul the British in North Africa,
the President calmly announced:

'In the future days which we seek to make secure, we look
forward to a world founded upon four essential human freedoms:

'The first is freedom of speech and expression—*everywhere
in the world.*'

Then came the freedom of every person to worship God
in his own way—'*everywhere in the world.*'

The third was freedom from want—'*everywhere in the
world.*'

Then freedom from fear, meaning the reduction of armaments 'to such a point and in such a thorough fashion that no
nation would be in a position to commit an act of physical
aggression against any neighbour—*anywhere in the world.*'

The phrases which I have italicised are the most astounding, and today the most heartbreaking. Was there really a time since the Garden of Eden when anybody could think such things could happen—*everywhere in the world?* Was there really a Franklin Roosevelt, among the many Franklin Roosevelts whom we watched with pleasure and apprehension, who could speak such words sincerely? If so, he was lucky to die long before the 1970s.

Furthermore, what did he mean by those future days 'which we seek to make secure'? How much 'seeking' were we doing in early 1941? We Americans were just beginning to argue about Lend-Lease. The British and the Greeks, plus some forlorn governments-in-Exile who had found refuge in London from their ruined countries, were seeking to avoid world-wide tyranny. Most of us in the United States were seeking more and larger motor-cars.

The Atlantic Charter of August, 1941, was another example of taking refuge from facts in a gabble of words. I was in London at the time and everybody was expecting something momentous from the meeting of President and Prime Minister in the North Atlantic. When the words came the let-down was saddening. These words seemed to presuppose the Second Coming of Christ before such good things could happen. What the British were awaiting was the second intervention of the United States.

6

Lend-Lease was not, I think, 'the most unsordid act'; but it was an astounding proof of Roosevelt's political tact and touch. Nothing less than Lend-Lease would suffice; nothing more was possible. Only the President could see how the necessary could come to pass. The bill (number 1776) was introduced into the House of Representatives and the Senate on January 10,

1941. After a stormy passage, and some amendments, it was accepted by House and Senate and signed by the President on March 11. On March 24 an appropriations bill for $7,000 million was accepted by the Congress. Senator Vandenberg, a leading opponent of Lend-Lease, admitted that 'the die is cast'.

The debates on Lend-Lease, in Congress and throughout the country, are almost frightening in retrospect. Since nobody really knew what lending or leasing meant and how, if at all, the charred bits of garden hose would return to America, and since the bill was presented in false colours as a means of keeping America out of the war, the defenders of the bill were in an awkward spot. In fact, most of the ardent supporters, in and out of Congress, knew that the bill meant war at some unspecified date but were told not to say so. Only grand old Senator Norris of Nebraska, the father of the Tennessee Valley Authority, said exactly what he thought in voting for the bill: that England was fighting America's war. This seemed to imply that America might some day fight her own war. And Secretary Stimson came close to the truth, in testifying before a Senate Committee: Hitler, he said, not Lend-Lease, would get us into the war.

A fortnight before the bill was presented to the House the President had spoken to the nation on the three radio networks. He admitted the facts but denied their implication. 'The whole purpose of your President', he said, 'is to keep you now, and your children later, and your grandchildren much later, out of last-ditch war for the preservation of American independence . . . Never since Jamestown and Plymouth Rock has our American civilisation been in such danger as now . . .

'The Nazi masters of Germany have made it quite clear that they intend not only to dominate all life and thought in their own country but also to enslave the whole of Europe and then to use the resources of Europe to dominate the rest of the world . . . The Axis not only admits but *proclaims* that there can be no ultimate peace between their philosophy of government and our philosophy of government . . .

'The American appeasers . . . tell you that the Axis powers are going to win anyway; that all this bloodshed in the world could be saved; that the United States might just as well throw its influence into the scale of a dictated peace, and get the best out of it that we can. They call it a "negotiated peace". Nonsense! Is it a negotiated peace if a gang of outlaws surrounds your community and on threat of extermination makes you pay tribute to save your own skins?'

This is what our group of war-mongers had been saying since June 10, 1940. But the President still refused to admit our conclusions. 'Thinking in terms of today and tomorrow,' he said in his broadcast, 'I make the direct statement to the American people that there is far less chance of the United States getting into war if we do all we can now to support the nations defending themselves against attack by the Axis than if we acquiesce in their defeat, submit tamely to an Axis victory, and wait our turn to be the object of attack in another war later . . . You can nail any talk about sending armies to Europe as deliberate untruth.'

Who were these 'nations defending themselves'? When the bill was passed and the huge appropriation made, the President sent lists of available goods to the British and the Greeks. It seemed a lot to ask a small island and a tiny nation to defend 'American independence' for us.

Even Churchill's well-schooled patience with Roosevelt sometimes gave way before the bland assumption that America was the benefactor who should be thanked rather than the beneficiary who should give thanks for all the blood the British (and by this time the Australians, Canadians and New Zealanders) were prepared to spend.

For example, when Churchill cabled to the President that he would seize the Azores if Spain were overrun, he was warned that he must make clear this was not for permanent occupation. 'We are far from wishing to add to our territory,' the Prime Minister answered, 'but only to preserve our life and perhaps yours.'

The President, through Robert Sherwood, asked our war-mongering group (which was now organised in every State and in every city except Milwaukee) to use all our efforts. We were the only unembarrassed defenders of Lend-Lease, although at times we felt we might be embarrassing the official defenders. When Senator Wheeler asked me: 'Are you not working for an undeclared war against Germany?' I answered, 'Certainly not. I am working for a declared war against Germany. Today, Lend-Lease is the best we can get.' The opponents of the bill and the war-mongers were the only ones free to say what they thought. When the President said the bill would make us 'the arsenal of democracy' we said this was wishful thinking: we would never be the arsenal of anything until we went to war. (During the first six months of 1941 the United States produced more automobiles than in any previous six-month period.) A funny argument, when the defenders of the bill were scoring off each other as much as off the enemy.

Then Churchill set the war-mongers back on their heels by his speech on February 9, 1941. Harry Hopkins was in London and he told the Prime Minister that the attack on the bill as a 'war measure' seemed to be winning over the defence that it was really a peace measure. Could the Prime Minister help? The answer was a speech on the radio which wound up:

'Here is the answer I will give President Roosevelt: put your confidence in us. Give us your faith and your blessing, and, under Providence, all will be well. We shall not fail or falter; and we shall not weaken or tire. Neither the sudden shock of battle, nor the long-drawn trials of vigilance and exertion will wear us down. Give us the tools, and we will finish the job.'

This was absurd but effective. It helped to pass the bill. It also made monkeys, for the time being, out of those of us who had been saying that the British could never win the war on their own.

Luckily the British invasion of Greece, and their rapid ejection therefrom, restored our credit (which was useful for money-raising) and raised the credit of Great Britain immeasurably, making her an heroic figure to a whole new group of Americans. I shall discuss that below.

By the spring of 1941 our pathetic little group of thirty which had signed 'A Summons to Speak Out' (on June 10, 1940) had grown into a nation-wide organisation under the name *Fight for Freedom*. After the Lend-Lease bill and the huge appropriation we thought we were on the edge of victory; but we were wrong. We still had to wait for Pearl Harbor.

The President had a private poll taken that spring on the question of war. For the first time a majority was in favour and a far larger majority thought war inevitable.[9] Yet the President waited. He still remembered Woodrow Wilson, and Wilson's divided nation. He probably felt that something would turn up to force Germany to make the first move and thus unite the country—perhaps U-boat attacks on our convoys to Iceland. I do not think he expected the Japanese to do the job. We all thought Japan would go down the coast of Asia against British and French possessions. This would not have helped Roosevelt with his last-ditch isolationists. The false sense of security created by Churchill's speech and the President's 'arsenal of democracy' found shocking expression in the House of Representatives, which renewed the conscription bill for the American armed forces by a majority of one. So the President and all the world waited.

By December the Administration knew where the first danger lay; but the rest of us still had our faces turned toward Germany. On December 7 I was at a lunch given by Spyros Skouras of Twentieth Century Fox—the idea being that I was to get a gift for *Fight for Freedom* from a rich woman. She

[9] I was shown the figures in 1942 when they no longer mattered and I was Special Assistant to the American Ambassador in London.

was spared the embarrassment of saying 'Yes' or 'No' because half-way through lunch we had the news of Pearl Harbor.

7

One fascination of the Lend-Lease debate is that it raises every awkward question about international relations within a continent-wide democracy. Can you tell the truth to 180 million people who are already angry and confused by their disagreements with each other and many of whom are further embittered by loves and hatreds inherited from their one-time mother-country? Had Americans been learning the trade of self-government for a thousand years, with few incursions of foreign blood, they would probably be less hysterical in their quarrels over mighty decisions such as war. In that dream-America a relatively sane man such as Senator Wheeler would not have charged Roosevelt with planning to 'plough under every fourth American boy'. And the President might not have been provoked by such nonsense into describing it 'as the most untruthful, as the most dastardly, unpatriotic thing . . . that has been said in public in my generation'. In the real America, however, these things were said.

When an amendment to the Lend-Lease bill was proposed, forbidding Lend-Lease aid to Russia at any time and under any circumstances, the Administration could not announce that it knew Germany planned to invade Russia before the end of the year. The Department of State had done its duty in warning Stalin, who paid no heed. There was no duty to tell the Germans how much the Department knew about their secrets. So the amendment was defeated by double-talk.

No moral question arises from this simple case; but what of Roosevelt's continual claim that the purpose of Lend-Lease was to keep America out of the war? I think the President believed that Lend-Lease would make a German victory impossible and that he hoped it would make American intervention unnecessary. For example, on January 7, 1941, he sent Harry Hopkins to London to see what was happening. Hopkins reported that the Germans were expected to invade before May 1, 1941. 'If Germany fails to win this invasion then I believe her sun is set.' At the same time Churchill was announcing, 'In order to win this war Hitler must destroy Great Britain.'

In retrospect all this may seem obvious. At the time, to those of us who visited the imperturbable island, it was just barely possible to believe that if sufficiently reinforced—fed, armed and aided in every way short of war—Britain might win alone. The possibility of believing this may justify the President in saying that Lend-Lease was a way of keeping his country out of a shooting war. He was at war with Germany; but it was still 'a qualified war'. If he had explained to his perplexed people every doubt, every possibility of disaster, he would have lost his Lend-Lease bill, lost Great Britain, and he would soon have been in a far more deadly war than the one he encountered. The bill was the best chance, such as it was, of staying out of war.

Should the President have stressed 'such as it was' more firmly? We of *Fight for Freedom*, who had always wanted war and were always confident it was coming, were happy to say that of course the bill meant war; but we were also happy to watch the President get the bill adopted. The revisionist historians who insist that Roosevelt always knew where he was heading, and always lied to the people, were either not present during those dark months or they have forgotten the ambiguities of democratic politics. They think all you need to do is to divine the truth and then follow it. This was the Wilsonian formula for defeat.

Stephen Benet, in *John Brown's Body*, makes Lincoln complain about the people who always knew exactly what he should say:

They come to me and talk about God's will . . .
God's will is Senator this and General that . . .

But all of them are sure they know God's will.
I am the only man who does not know it.

Lincoln, too, could be most devious; yet he saved the country. Who can tell where to draw the line?

Commenting on the election of 1940, Dr Kimball asks: 'Must a candidate dwell on the possibility of war when doing so he would probably elect people whose policies might, in his view, endanger national security? . . . In that sense democracy may be a suicide pact.' The same may apply to the battle for Lend-Lease. I do not know. It is an unhappy question. It cannot be answered by simple abuse of Roosevelt.

Another reason for hoping, longing, that Lend-Lease might be sufficient, another reason for self-deception even in high places, was Japan's adherence to the European Axis September 27, 1940. Few Americans noted at the time, or remember today, what this Tripartite Pact meant; namely, that if Japan or Germany or Italy got into war with the United States the other two would join. So the United States navy, according to Admiral Morison, 'would be fighting a two-ocean war with a much less than one-ocean fleet'. In June 1940, just after the German occupation of Paris, Admiral Stark (Chief of Naval Operations) had asked Congress for $4,000 million. The money was appropriated and it would more than double the size of the fleet, but only in blue-print for the time being. 'Dollars', said Admiral Stark sadly, 'cannot buy yesterday.' Admiral Morison commented: 'For two years at least, the Americans would be vulnerable in the event of a German victory in Europe.'

Before signing the Tripartite Pact the Japanese had made clear what they wanted when they fought America: 'The former German islands under mandate to Japan; French Indo-China and Pacific Islands, Thailand, British Malaya, British Borneo, Dutch East Indies, Burma, Australia, New Zealand, India, etc.' The signing of this Tripartite Pact, wrote Professor Samuel Flagg Bemis of Yale, had 'globe-shaking repercussions, convulsing diplomacy from Washington to Chungking'.

Incidentally, and much to the relief of Washington, the

promise to declare war on the United States if Japan struck is the only inconvenient promise which Hitler and Mussolini ever kept. Had Britain fallen, the fate of America with half her navy still in blue-print would not have been pleasing. And the reason Washington was happy about the declarations of war was that in March, 1941, the British and American Chiefs of Staff had met quietly in Washington and agreed that if America got into the war the policy of both countries would be 'Germany first'. Japan should be contained and dealt with in good time when the Germans were finished.

At the Washington meeting it was agreed that the American and British Chiefs of Staff would come together as the Combined Chiefs of Staff should the United States become involved. The Combined Chiefs would make strategic plans for all the Allied armed forces. (This proved a blessing, preventing most of the friction and misunderstandings which had been a curse in the First World War.) Furthermore, the United States had begun to recreate an Atlantic fleet in February, 1941, and it was agreed that, war or no war, this fleet should help in escorting Atlantic convoys to a meeting point south of Iceland where the Royal Navy took over. Before long the President gave orders to shoot on sight any ship interfering with American convoys. This led to naval skirmishes and to the sinking of an American destroyer with the loss of 115 lives.

In spite of increasing involvement in the Atlantic, which included an American protectorate over Greenland and an American occupation of Iceland, Pearl Harbor might have thwarted the plans made in March by the Chiefs of Staff. Isolationism was silenced, but even Roosevelt could have had difficulty in directing his country's wrath against Germany first, especially since the isolationists, including men like Lindbergh, had been preaching for two years that Hitler was warm-hearted and benign toward the United States. The German declaration of war took care of that nonsense.

We may never know why some historians pretend that Pearl Harbor was a plot by Roosevelt. Professor Bemis wrote in the

New York Times: 'Now it is a most extraordinary phenomenon in historiography that none of the American revisionist writers on World War II mentions the key document quoted above (i.e. Japan's demands for joining the Tripartite Pact). The earlier ones, of course, did not know about it because it became available only in the evidence submitted before the Tokyo tribunals in 1948 . . . Since then historians who ignore this truly remarkable and revealing document and other evidence brought forth at Tokyo and Berlin lay themselves open to the accusation of concealing essential evidence that disproves the charge that Roosevelt clandestinely plotted with Churchill the dramatic war of the Pacific. It was the Japanese leaders who secretly plotted that holocaust . . . And it was Hitler and the Nazi leaders who plotted the war in Europe. Revisionist writers do not deny this; they merely gloss it over, or say that it was none of our business.'

The President had long known the danger from Japan. In September, 1940 (before his third-term election), he had placed an embargo on iron and steel scrap, but not on oil. When his wife protested against supplying the Japanese with oil he replied that 'the real answer which you *cannot* use is that if we forbid oil shipments Japan . . . may be driven by actual necessity to a descent on the Dutch East Indies.'

In December, 1940, Ambassador Joseph Grew—eight years in Tokyo and one of the wisest men in the American Foreign service—warned Roosevelt that Japan meant war. 'Sooner or later,' wrote Grew, 'unless we are prepared . . . to withdraw bag and baggage from the entire sphere of "greater East Asia including the South Seas" (which God forbid), we are bound eventually to come to a head-on clash with Japan . . . Only if they (the Japanese) become certain that we mean to fight if called upon to do so will our preliminary measures stand some chance of proving effective and of removing the necessity for war—the old story of Sir Edward Grey in 1914.'

This was written almost a year before Pearl Harbor and is another document which the revisionists prefer to ignore.

Grew was not writing about a country which could be tricked by a guileful President into an unwanted war.

Those of us who have been told, after two wars, that the whole thing was a mistake or else our own fault, must be allowed to lose our patience sometimes.

VI
North Africa, Greece and Lend-Lease

1

When the defeat of France became certain, Mussolini brought Italy into the war hoping to pick up the scraps which dropped from the Fuehrer's table. If the British navy had believed what the Committee of Imperial Defence reported at the time of Abyssinia, Mussolini's move might have been fatal to Britain in the Mediterranean and North Africa. Luckily, the sea-going navy believed nothing of the sort. There is a difference between sitting at home and predicting, fearful lest a ray of optimism may lead to a defeat which will then be laid on your own shoulders, and plunging through the seas in a ship stripped for battle. There is also a difference between the Italian navy on paper (which is all the men at home can assess) and the Italian navy at war.

Since the Italian armed forces come out badly in my narrative, and since I know the valour of Italians, I must turn aside to raise two questions. First: What were the Italians fighting for on June 10, 1940?

(a) Mussolini? Not an inspiring sight and he had been too long on the scene. The silver-gilt was wearing thin and the Italians, who have seen everything for two thousand years, are cynical about fakes.

(b) Plunder? The same cynicism told them that if there were any rich pluckings the Germans would have them. And the Italians were no longer ruffian-adventurers like the terrible *condottiere* of Verrochio's statue in Venice, to whom any plunder would be better than none. Besides, they rather liked the English and hated Germans.

(c) Italy? Why fight for Italy since nobody had threatened Italy except by asking her to stay out of the war?

This raises my second question: What is Italy? A beautiful and varied land and the repository of much of the loveliest art and architecture. The heir to two millennia of conquests and reconquests, of petty rivalries and of great betrayals and hates. A place where people have watched everything and suffered everything from the days of the Roman *latifundia* to the days when 'Christ Stopped at Eboli'. Such people are not easily impressed. Finally, Italy is a recent mish-mash of Sicilians (who have Greece and Carthage in their blood), Calabrians (who used to be raided and raped by the Saracens), Neapolitans, Romans, Tuscans, Venetians and many others. In 1913 my tutor, who spoke pure Tuscan, could scarcely be understood in Venice. Radio and television are changing this; but only yesterday there was little unity of language and less unity of blood between a Sicilian and a Milanese.

So who exactly were the Italians whom Mussolini hurled carelessly into the great war of the West? They were a half-integrated people, the newest of great nations, industrious and formidable at home, wholly disillusioned of any thought that good could come from yet another war. They were, in their various corners of Italy, the heirs to more history than anyone else in Europe has suffered.[1] They were, therefore, the least likely of all Europeans to be beguiled by hopes. They were also the descendants of great poets, artists, philosophers and men of science. So why die in the desert or in the mountains of Greece for Mussolini and a pack of Germans? I feel this question was in the minds of many Italian warriors. It

[1] The Greeks were withdrawn from history, or hibernating within history, during four centuries of Turkish rule.

is not a question which leads on toward heroism; but it may lead toward cruelty. If you have no heart for the fight you are easily frightened, and frightened troops are notoriously cruel.

In any case Mussolini did thrust his people into the war on June 10, thereby destroying his own régime and hastening the end of Hitler's. Many people thought at the time that this 'stab in the back' marked Britain's darkest hour; but nothing could have been luckier for Churchill or more baneful for Hitler.

The Italians had troops in Libya and East Africa, more than half a million. General Wavell (Commander-in-Chief, Middle East) had 50,000 soldiers with which to guard Egypt and Sudan. This little army was hard to reinforce since the British still took the Italian navy seriously and sent men and supplies by the Cape route—down the interminable west coast of Africa and up the east coast into the Red Sea. Impudently, while France was falling, the British did send 7,000 troops to Wavell. They did not reach Egypt until late August. This was a testimony to Churchill's belief that if Egypt fell all might fall and to the War Cabinet's view that the war was a global contest and that the fall of France and even of England might one day be rectified—and also to the fact that the Cape route was too slow. The Italian fleet must be diminished. This was done on November 11, 1940, when Admiral Cunningham's Fleet Air Arm struck at the fortified harbour of Taranto. Three out of six battleships were sunk. Two cruisers and two fleet auxiliaries were severely damaged. Only twenty-one British bombers were involved. The Italians were now inferior in the Mediterranean.

2

The title of this chapter may seem far-fetched, but not to anyone who tried to raise money in America to support the Lend-Lease bill. A continent-wide campaign with full-page advertisements in twenty-five newspapers, a few debates with national hook-ups on the radio, a number of speakers travelling the country arguing before local audiences: this is vastly expensive. Between us, *Fight for Freedom* and *The Committee to Defend America by Aiding the Allies* could not do the minimum job to take our story into every town and village. Unhappily, the last-ditch isolationists of *America First* could do the minimum job, and more. They had all the money they could use. Their only problem was to be clever enough to use it wisely. These were the people whose motto was 'You CAN do business with Hitler'. If you could believe that, you might feel it would be easier to do your business with one group (such as the Nazis) who owned the whole of Europe rather than with lots of little untidy nations of free people.

Maybe none of our efforts, pro or con, made any difference. Maybe the wand of the magician in the White House would have been sufficient; but the magician wasn't sure, or he wouldn't have asked us to stir up support from the eastern to the western oceans and especially between the Appalachians and the Sierra Nevada. So from January 10 to March 10, 1941, I was visiting the big cities of America begging for money for *Fight for Freedom*. These were the months when the debate on Lend-Lease raged. These were the months when the British War Cabinet stopped Wavell and O'Connor from their headlong trampling over the Italians in North Africa in order to prepare to keep their promise to help the Greeks.

After two months of redeployment the first British troops landed in Greece on March 7, 1941. The Lend-Lease bill was signed by the President on March 11. Assuming, as he himself did assume, that the President needed help in getting his way, the two events may be related.

3

Hitler, who was surprisingly forgiving with Mussolini but who did not overrate him, had allotted one simple task to the Italians. They were to remove the British from Egypt and from the Suez Canal. Don't try anything else, Hitler instructed his partner. Don't do anything which could waste your forces. Just take the Canal and cut the British off from the Middle East and from the quick route to India and Singapore. Surely, the Fuehrer seems to have thought, even an Italian army can do this while the British at home are being cowed by the Luftwaffe; but nothing went easily for Hitler after the fall of France. The Luftwaffe failed; the Italians failed; and then Mussolini upset the applecart by invading Greece.

In September, 1940, Graziani had moved his large army eastward from Libya against the British. According to Rommel, the British 'had nothing in Egypt capable of holding the Italians before Alexandria'. They may have had nothing; but the Italians had something worse: an army wholly unfit for the desert. Mussolini boasted that he had sent to Libya an army of 14,000 officers and 327,000 troops and great stores of material. Rommel comments: 'The harsh truth was that this army fell a long way short of the standard required by modern warfare. It was designed for a colonial war against insurgent tribesmen . . . Its worst feature was the fact that a great part of the Italian army consisted of non-motorised infantry. In the North African desert, non-motorised troops are of practically no value against a motorised enemy.'

Graziani moved, scarcely opposed, as far as Sidi Barrani which is some 200 miles from Alexandria. There the Italians sat for weeks and months: fortifying, building a road along the coast, bringing up stores and organising water supplies, doing everything except fighting, and thus giving the British time to assemble forces from all over the Empire and to bring mechanised troops and an air force and their latest tanks into Egypt. The Duce's chance of taking an undefended Egypt was lost forever.

The chance would not have been lost had Graziani's army been German, as Rommel was soon to prove; but Hitler had not yet felt the need to send Germans to the aid of Graziani. He still assumed that an Italian army four times the size of a British army could make some progress.

4

Hitler visited Spain in October, 1940, for his famous interview with Franco. He got sweet words but no help and no firm promises. The Caudillo was not sure the British were finished. They (in the person of their Ambassador at Madrid, Sir Samuel Hoare) still seemed unperturbed. Hitler was asking for favours. The British were asking for nothing but neutrality. Spain was asking a huge price for gambling on the Nazis— hence Hitler's comment that he would rather have his teeth pulled than sit again with Franco.

The American Army of Occupation found in Germany the 1940 correspondence between the Fuehrer, the Duce and the Caudillo. The documents prove two things: first, in Hoare's words, 'that Franco was throughout the period of my mission determined to enter the war on the side of the Axis provided that he was not involved in any serious fighting'; second, that each of the three dictators wanted the whole of North Africa and that there was no honour among these thieves. 'Fortunately for us,' writes Lord Templewood (Sir Samuel Hoare), 'their hatred of the democracies was made subservient to their jealousy of each other.' Fortunately for us, one might add, our enemies are even more obtuse than ourselves—else what price democracy?

On August 8, 1940, the German Ambassador in Madrid sent a signal to Berlin: 'Operation Gibraltar. The Spanish Government declares itself ready, under certain conditions, to give up its position as a "non-belligerent" State and to enter the war on the side of Germany and Italy.' This was the day of Goering's *Adlertag*, the start of the Battle of Britain—just the day to join the Axis had Goering succeeded. Yet Franco's 'certain conditions' were startling. They suggest that he thought Hitler might be involved in a long, exhausting war and that now was the time to take advantage of his friend. His demands were: first, Gibraltar, French Morocco, Oran, 'the enlargement of the Rio de Oro and of the colonies in the Gulf of Guinea'; second, 'making available military and other assistance required for carrying on the war'.

Over this last demand the talks at Hendaye foundered. Hitler was happy to promise away other people's colonies even if he intended, later, to keep them for himself; but 'assistance', he learned, meant repairing and then re-arming and then supplying the Spanish army. The German Ambassador, in his innocence, had on August 8 urged Berlin to accept Franco's terms. He could not have divined what 'assistance' meant. On August 15 Franco told Mussolini the truth—all hedged round with affection and boasts of what Spain had done for the New Order. What he needed in order to fight, he implied, was everything.

The Duce's reply was less affectionate. 'Dear Franco, It is clear to me that Spain, after three years of Civil War, needed a long period of recuperation, but events will not permit it, and your domestic economic condition will not get worse when you change from non-belligerency to intervention.'

Franco almost took the plunge in January, 1941; but the disasters to Mussolini's armies held him back. He simply could not afford to fight, though he longed to be in at the death. His position was tricky. He asked for Gibraltar, Morocco, Oran, etc. in return for his aid, and then he asked for all the armaments he needed in order to give that aid. No wonder Hitler found him irksome.

On his way to Hendaye Hitler had talked to Laval about French collaboration. On his way home he talked with both Laval and Pétain at Montoire. Some say Pétain offered French troops against the British; but this seems unlikely. His own vague explanation to the French people may well be correct if one could understand what it means. 'It is freely that I accepted the Fuehrer's invitation,' he said; 'I did not have to put up with any *Diktat* or pressure from him. A collaboration has been envisaged between our two countries. I have accepted the principle of it. The details will be discussed later . . . This collaboration must be sincere. It must exclude all idea of aggression. It must carry with it a patient and confident effort.'

What were the British people to make of that? Did they have still another enemy, or didn't they? And what of the French fleet at Toulon? Events were to show that Pétain didn't mean much of anything. In June, 1941, the British and the Free French invaded Syria. Vichy troops resisted and were beaten; but Pétain refused help from the German air force, thus seeming to rule out all forms of military collaboration. And in 1942, after a stormy meeting with Goering, Pétain reproached Germany for betraying the 'good will' expressed at Montoire: 'I understood that collaboration implied treating between equals,' he said. 'If instead there is a victor above and a vanquished below, there is what you call a *Diktat*, and what we call *la loi de la plus fort.*' What did the broken old man expect? He still could not see that he was dealing with Genghis Khan.

5

A few days after Montoire, on October 28, 1940, Mussolini attacked Greece and upset Hitler's plans for 'Operation

Felix': an assault on Gibraltar by three German divisions (with or without Spanish aid), also an air attack on the Portuguese Cape Verde Islands. Even if Spain could not fight for Gibraltar, Franco had to give permission for the Germans to pass; otherwise Hitler's three divisions might find themselves, like Napoleon's troops, balked by an enraged peasantry.[2]

'Operation Felix', had Hitler listened to reason, might have been on such a scale that neither Franco nor the angry Spaniards could have interfered. Admiral Raeder and Goering, in agreement for the first and last time, had been urging Hitler to make a major campaign after seizing Gibraltar; to secure north-west Africa with the help of Vichy, then to take Egypt along with the frail Italians, then to push north through Palestine and Syria to Turkey. This was the alternative to the attack on Russia and would have involved large German armies which could have brushed the Spaniards aside, hostile or not. As Raeder and Goering urged, here was the quick way to remove the British from the whole Mediterranean world, cutting them off from their Empire. Then the U-boats, with the help of the Luftwaffe, would starve England to death. Hitler, forever ignorant of the meaning of sea-power, said the plan was a distraction and that he must concentrate on the land-mass of Russia. Meanwhile Franco vetoed even the small, three-division version of 'Operation Felix'.

On December 7, 1940, Admiral Canaris, in the name of the Fuehrer, told Franco that all was ready. The Germans would cross the frontier on December 10. Gibraltar would prove more vulnerable than the Fortress Eben Emael in Belgium and would be taken by the same methods and the same paratroops. Franco refused. The Italians were being mauled in North Africa and in Greece. The British had beaten the Luftwaffe

[2] Whatever Franco's twists and turnings, the Spanish people did not want war, or Germans. They probably did not want Franco either; but a foreign army, uninvited, would have let them indulge their accumulated hatreds.

in daytime and did not seem overimpressed by the nightly blitz. And Hitler had not given Spain the arms with which to fight. Franco longed for Gibraltar. He still thought Germany would win; but until he could set a date for victory he dared not join the Axis. Mussolini had thought the war was over when he blustered his way into it on June 10—and look at the Duce now.

The Duce was indeed a sad sight. In order to show that he, too, could overawe small nations he had sent an ultimatum to General Metaxas at 3 a.m. on October 28. This melodrama was supposed to look Hitlerian but merely looked rude. Metaxas received the Italian Minister in his dressing-gown and was given an ultimatum: Italy must occupy strategic points in Greece until the end of the war.

'Oxi' (No), said Metaxas. This word may have changed history. 'Let there be no doubt about it,' wrote Sir Compton Mackenzie, with slight but pardonable exaggeration, 'if Greece had accepted the Italian ultimatum in October, 1940, there might have been no battle of El Alamein to fight in October, 1942, and what is more, Moscow would probably have fallen in October, 1941. It was meet that the most powerful foe democracy has had to face should find his doom in the land where democracy was born.' These were early days. Countless people found their doom before that 'most powerful foe' faced the meaning of 'Oxi'. Yet Sir Compton may be right. Greek intransigence, long before Churchill dared use his famous words in 1942, may have been 'the end of the beginning'. For Mussolini, it was the beginning of the end.

Hitler thought he had soothed and awed the Balkans, in preparation for the invasion of Russia. Now, seven months before that intended invasion, the Duce had aroused the whole quarrelsome peninsula, and for no reason except a jealous desire to show that he was as dangerous and unpredictable as Hitler. In the Fuehrer's plans, as we have seen, the Italians were supposed to scatter the tiny British Army in North Africa and to invade Egypt. That was the one use the

Germans could see for them. Now they had stumbled into the most delicate trouble-spot in Europe. Bulgaria and Yugoslavia had designs on Greece. And the British had made promises to Greece.

Glumly and slowly Hitler made ready to send German troops to North Africa, since no one could expect the Italians to invade Greece and Egypt at the same time. Ten German divisions were set aside to attack Greece if the British dared to keep their promise. And German forces in Rumania were increased.

In spite of this wayward interference with German plans, Hitler remained polite to Mussolini, wishing him well in Greece and offering him paratroops if he needed them, later, in Crete. After Franco's maundering and Pétain's vague 'collaboration', the Fuehrer may have thought that any ally was better than none. If so, he was wrong.

Years later, a few months before his suicide, Hitler was reminiscing about the early days of the war. Bormann took recordings as Hitler talked. The Fuehrer agreed with the revisionist historians that the war was basically Chamberlain's fault. Chamberlain had fooled Hitler at Munich and delayed the war for a year. But for the siren-song from Birmingham, Hitler would have taken the whole of eastern Europe in 1938 and nobody would have objected. The gentle peace of death would have descended.

Turning from the wicked Prime Minister to the disappointing war, Hitler admitted that his 'unshakable friendship' for the Duce had been a dire mistake. The Italians were a nuisance from start to finish. They had lost every campaign and by invading Greece and drawing Britain into the Balkans they had delayed Germany for six weeks in her attack on Russia. 'Our Italian ally', he summed up, 'has been a source of embarrassment to us everywhere.'

6

An example of this embarrassment was Graziani's army at
Sidi Barrani which sat quietly for months, planning for its
future comfort but not, it seemed, for war. During this restful
period, three armoured regiments arrived to strengthen Wavell;
an Indian and an Australian division and a skeleton division
from New Zealand. The Italians were now only three to one
in strength, and inferior in tanks, so on December 7, 1940,
Wavell and O'Connor decided to see what was happening in
Graziani's camp. They did not plan to do much harm; but they
found themselves in an astonishing race of 500 miles along
the coast of Cyrenaica, until they were within striking distance of Tripolitania. Meanwhile they acquired countless
prisoners, tanks and guns. 'Never has so much been surrendered by so many to so few,' said Anthony Eden.

By early February, 1941, Graziani's army was destroyed.
The road was open to Tripoli; but on February 12, Churchill
told Wavell to leave the minimum holding-force in Cyrenaica
and to prepare the largest possible force (on land and in the
air) for the support of Greece.

The British had promised all possible help if Greece were
attacked. Metaxas did not want help. He thought, correctly,
that the Germans would never allow the British a foothold
in the Balkans. Metaxas died on January 29 and the new
Prime Minister asked the British to redeem their promise. His
people were determined to rid the place of Italians and he
wanted all the help he could get. On March 7, 1941, the first
of 50,000 British and Imperial troops landed in Greece. On
April 6, ten German divisions, with more than their normal
quota of tanks, invaded.

Meanwhile, on February 6, Rommel wrote: 'In view of the
highly critical situation of our Italian allies, two German

divisions—one light and one panzer—were to be sent to Libya to their help. I was to take command of this German Afrika Korps . . . The middle of February would see the arrival of the first German troops in Africa; the movement of the 5th Light Division would be complete by mid-April and of the 15th Panzer Division by the end of May.' On the same day he wrote to his wife: 'It'll be months before anything materialises.'

The Germans might have been sorry for such uncharacteristic slowness had not the British withdrawn most of their troops from Cyrenaica a few days after Rommel's appointment. On February 11 Rommel noted: 'The latest news from Africa was very grave. Wavell had taken Benghazi, destroyed the last Italian armoured division south of the town and was about to advance into Tripolitania. In fact no serious further resistance by the Italians was to be expected. It was not impossible that the next few days would see the arrival of the leading British troops in the environs of Tripoli.' By the end of May there might have been no place in North Africa for Rommel's 15th Panzer Division, short of Algeria. There the Vichy-faithful troops might have been as ugly and unhelpful as they were to the Americans eighteen months later.

In fact the Germans were ahead of their timetable as usual, and by April Rommel was pushing the diminished British forces out of Cyrenaica. The British and Commonwealth troops were thrown out of Greece in the same month, with the loss of 13,000 men, mostly prisoners, and of all their tanks. Then they were thrown out of Crete on the last day of May. Military historians have judged the Greek adventure harshly.

Someone said earlier in the war that the British, once known as a nation of shopkeepers, now seemed to be a nation of undertakers. Every nation they sought to help was quickly abolished: Poland, Norway, Holland, Belgium, France and now Greece and Crete. Yet the last losses were by no means ignominious, and they played their part in the defeat of Hitler.

The British presence in Greece (plus the Yugoslav uprising

at the end of March, 1941, which overthrew the pro-Axis Government) forced Hitler to conquer the Balkans and to delay his attack on Russia by four to six weeks. Had the Germans arrived on the outskirts of Moscow a month sooner, the capital must have fallen. Liddell Hart suggests that the weather would have delayed Hitler in any case. This we cannot prove; but we do know that Hitler had set May 15 as the date for his invasion, and that toward the end of March the date was deferred for a month and then set for June 22. Field-Marshal von Kleist seems certain of the reason for the delay. 'It is true', he said, 'that the forces employed in the Balkans were not large . . . but the proportion of tanks employed there was high. The bulk of the tanks that came under me for the offensive against the Russian front in southern Poland had taken part in the Balkan offensive, and needed overhaul . . . A large number of them had driven as far south as the Peloponnese and had to be brought back all that way.'

We also know that Hitler was shocked by the casualties among his parachute troops in Crete. His generals could not persuade him to try any more island-adventures in the Mediterranean—a godsend to the British and the Maltese.

Another odd result of the British aid-to-Greece was the help it gave in America to those who were raising funds to promote war on Germany and to support aid-to-Britain. Far from being seen as just another failure, the support of Greece was saluted in the United States as a gallant promise-keeping in a world that had seemed to be corrupted by German promise-breaking.

The first troops landed in Greece in time to influence the Congressional vote on Lend-Lease. More than ever the British seemed worth aiding, although those of us who were impatient for war seemed no nearer to our goal. After Greece, however, we had more money to fight with. Not only did rich American Greeks suddenly open their purses, but something symbolic, mythologically potent, adhered to the name and the half-known history of Greece. The fate of the rest of Europe, and what it meant, was brought alive to many

Americans by the fate of Greece—brushed aside and then enslaved lest she become a minor nuisance to the Fuehrer's terrible plans.

Since Lend-Lease did not, unhappily, lead America into war, those of us in the war-party whose job it was to raise money for propaganda had still to travel the country making speeches and asking for cash. After Greece, the anti-British taunts and heckling diminished notably. Since millions of Americans are only two or three generations out of Germany or Ireland, our audience never lacked people to cry out against the sins of England or to proclaim her hopeless record in this war and her moral decrepitude. Her sins against Ireland were still dragged out monotonously; but after Greece her war record and her morals were mentioned less and less.

On April 27 Churchill explained to his people the loss of still more troops and still more tanks and still more ships in yet another evacuation: 'When we reached Benghazi and what was left of Mussolini's legions scurried back along the dusty road to Tripoli, a call was made upon us which we could not resist. Let me tell you about that call . . . In their mortal peril the Greeks turned to us for succour. Strained as were our resources, we could not say them nay. By a solemn guarantee . . . Great Britain had promised them her help. They declared that they would fight for their native soil . . . even if we left them to their fate. But we could not do that. There are rules against that kind of thing, and to break those rules would be fatal to the honour of the British Empire, without which we could neither hope nor deserve to win this hard war . . . So an important part of the mobile portions of the Army of the Nile was sent to Greece in fulfilment of our pledge.'

In the light of today's abounding cynicism toward politicians, this may seem like just another excuse for a failed campaign; but it did not sound like that to Americans in the spring of 1941. And Churchill the romantic may have believed briefly that he was telling the whole truth, that it was merely a question of honour. The truth was more complicated.

On February 12, as we have seen, the Army of the Nile was told to stop chasing Italians and prepare to help Greece. Then Anthony Eden and General Dill[3] went to the Middle East to sound out the Turks and Greeks and Yugoslavs as to prospects. The Turks would do nothing unless attacked. The Greeks would fight with or without help. The Yugoslav Government was still pro-Axis. Churchill warned Eden not to commit Britain if he foresaw another Norway; but Eden and General Dill were hopeful. On March 6 Sir Alexander Cadogan noted in his diary: 'Anthony has evidently committed us up to the hilt. Telegram this morning gives text of agreement signed with the Greeks . . . Cabinet at 6 . . . P.M. evidently thinks we can't go back on Anthony and Dill.' And on March 7: 'Cabinet at 12, which practically decided to go ahead in Balkans. On a nice balance, I think this is right.' So Churchill assured Eden that the Cabinet had assumed 'the fullest responsibility', and the first British troops landed the same day. Aid to Greece had been decided, not purely on a question of honour but also on a careful calculation of chances.[4] What mattered in the United States, however, was how it looked and sounded at the time.

7

Great events may have bizarre by-products. The British defeat in Greece persuaded Rudolf Hess that the time had come for him to fly to Britain. Thanks to James Douglas-Hamilton's book[5] we now know the full story of Hess, a story which

[3] Chief of the Imperial General Staff.

[4] This was more than a fortnight before the Yugoslav anti-Axis revolt, the quick suppression of which made the hopes of the Greek and British armies even more meagre.

[5] *Motive for a Mission* (see Bibliography).

justifies Churchill's reflection: 'Whatever may be the moral guilt of a German who stood near to Hitler, Hess had in my view atoned for this by his completely devoted and fanatic deed of lunatic benevolence. He came to us of his own free will . . . He was a medical and not a criminal case.'

'Lunatic benevolence' is the phrase for Hess. 'Benevolence' because he had no other purpose than to stop the war between Germany and Britain, thus serving both Hitler and the world. 'Lunatic' because he had nothing new to offer. He thought that if he could tell the King of England what a good man Hitler was, and that the Nazis only wanted Europe and had no harsh thought about the British Empire, everyone would be happy and shake hands. Hitler would welcome Hess home as a devoted hero, after which the Germans would demolish Russia while the British smiled from the sidelines. This was not a sane view of life in 1941; but it is a view which Hitler himself had recently shared. Now that we have all the facts, we can learn something about the breakdown of Anglo-Nazi relations by asking how on earth Hess got that way.

First, Hess was one of Hitler's two deputies and thus the second man in the Reich, except that within that jungle of sly beasts Number 2 must have the power to kick Number 3 in the face should No. 3 show signs of climbing the ladder. Hess was not sure he still had that power, so here was one motive for creating peace with England—a peace which Hitler had sought on the same terms and had failed to get. If Hess could explain the generosity of those terms, first to the Duke of Hamilton and then to the King, all should be well.

Second, Hess had studied under Karl Haushofer, the inventor of the German version of geopolitics and of the sinister concept, *Lebensraum*. Thus Hess never thought it odd that the Nazis planned to occupy and depopulate half of European Russia.

Third, Hess became friend and protector of Haushofer's son, Albrecht—a brilliant man whom Hess made an 'honorary Aryan' and also an adviser on foreign affairs to Ribbentrop.

Albrecht's advice was good and unwelcome since he was passionately against an Anglo-German war. He kept explaining to Ribbentrop that the Germans would lose. Also he had met Lord Clydesdale, later the Duke of Hamilton, to whose estate Hess sought to fly. What Albrecht tried to teach the dull-minded Hess can be shown in two quotations:

(a) In 1937, after a trip to the United States, Albrecht wrote, 'Whether you are in San Francisco or Washington you are aware that a fight for existence by Britain would not leave the United States in the role of impartial observers . . . Whoever gets into conflict with Britain should know that America too will be among his opponents, in spite of all neutrality laws.'[6]

(b) After Godesberg, when Hitler had threatened and Chamberlain had been weak, Albrecht warned that Britain would not in the end give way. Daringly for an 'honorary Aryan' whose job it was to advise the unadvisable Ribbentrop, he wrote in the *Zeitschrift für Geopolitik:* 'The whole of British history, the whole grim history of its conflicts with rival powers, from Spain, via Holland and France to Germany and Russia, would have to be rewritten if one wanted to believe that present-day British armaments are merely a bluff or that the Anglo-Saxon world could be bluffed for ever.'

So Hess half-believed, with Albrecht Haushofer, that war with Britain would be fatal to Germany in the end; but he could not persuade his beloved Fuehrer of this. And Hess had access, through Albrecht, to what he thought was the seat of power in Britain. Dukes, he imagined, must hob-nob with the King. And the King, he seemed to think, could tell his Government what to do. (This Duke was commanding an R.A.F. fighter-sector in the east of Scotland.)

In September, 1940, at Hess's request, Albrecht tried to get in touch with the Duke of Hamilton through friends in a neutral country. Hitler may well have known of this attempt

[6] I and my friends wished that our fellow-countrymen could see the point as clearly as this.

to talk peace; but nothing came of it. Hess decided that when the time came he must fly to Scotland, find the Duke, and save the world by himself. He tried in January, 1941; but bad weather frustrated him. Then while Britain was victorious in North Africa, he was afraid he might make Germany sound weak or frightened; but when Britain was thrown out of Greece he felt his time had come. On May 10, 1941 (the last day of the Blitz on London and an exact year after Hitler had attacked France and the Low Countries), he made his leap into the dark.

When Hess baled out over Lanarkshire he was captured and taken to Glasgow. Since he was in uniform he was not shot. Instead, the astonished Duke of Hamilton was asked to leave his post of duty and if possible identify this strange prisoner who had given a false name but who claimed to know the Duke. Hamilton had never seen Hess; but he was quickly convinced that the prisoner really was Hess, so he flew south to see the Prime Minister. Churchill was spending the week-end at Ditchley Park in Oxfordshire. He was just finishing dinner and looking forward to seeing a motion picture. Hess, who was expecting to change history and become a national hero, would have found the meeting between Churchill and the Duke an anti-climax: 'Do you mean to tell me that the Deputy Fuehrer of Germany is in our hands?' Hamilton said that he was reasonably sure.

'Well,' said the Prime Minister, 'Hess or no Hess I am going to see the Marx Brothers.'

8

Six weeks after the deluded Hess put himself into prison for life, the Germans invaded Russia. The lonely year was ended. The British had once more done their wholesome job of seeing to it that no one conquered Europe. Yet on June 22, 1941, few people felt that the loneliness was over.

The experts thought Russia would die quickly. And the experts failed to foresee that the United States would soon be reminded of the price of power by Japan. In keeping with all their earlier predictions, the experts were madly wrong.

Anthony Eden was at Chequers with Churchill on the evening of June 21. Both of them knew that in Russia the balloon was about to go up. 'Our advisers were pessimistic about what the Russians could do,' Eden records; 'Cripps excused the Soviet appeasement of the Nazis on the ground of their extreme weakness . . . He had told the War Cabinet on June 16 that the prevailing view in diplomatic circles in Moscow was that Russia could not hold out against Germany for more than three or four weeks. Dill . . . hoped for a few weeks longer, but thought that we should be unwise to count on more than six or seven.'

In America the President and the Department of State received the same unworthy advice. And on that Sunday I and my war-mongering friends were meeting in Princeton, at the Institute for Advanced Study, to hear from our non-official experts what we could do most usefully in the way of promoting war. None of us amateurs knew about 'Barbarossa', the code name for the invasion of Russia. At noon we heard of the world-shaking invasion. Our own experts matched those of the British and American Governments, giving the Russians from three weeks to three months. And 'three months' was frowned on by some as being needlessly hopeful.

'The hinge of fate' had swung our way, though we did not know it. Robert Sherwood and I had an example of the global change later on that same Sunday. We were speaking in Harlem for 'Fight for Freedom' before the first black group we had been able to recruit. (Black Americans were not over-eager to help the white man save his skin.) Entering the Golden Gate Ballroom we were picketed by black Communists. We were 'fascist beasts,' slaves of Wall Street and dupes of the

British. Two hours later we were cheered as we left the ball-room. Our oratory had not saved the day. The new Party Line from Moscow had reached Harlem, explaining that we were no longer beasts but prophets and that all good men must now join us in working for war. We were glad to be re-prieved from beasthood; yet the sudden somersault made us thoughtful.

General de Gaulle commented on the same macabre head-over-heels in London. 'Whereas the Moscow radio had not ceased to hold forth against "the English imperialists" and their "Gaullist mercenaries" up to the very moment when the Ger-man tanks crossed the Russian frontier, the Moscow wave-lengths were heard pouring forth encomia on Churchill and de Gaulle an hour afterwards.'

Churchill was more severe. He did his duty and praised the devil on the B.B.C., and promised all possible aid; but he re-corded that Stalin, in June of 1941, was 'at once a callous, a crafty and an ill-informed giant'. Churchill knew that as recently as November, 1940, when Hitler was bargaining with Molotov as to who got what at the end of the war, the Fuehrer explained that the British Empire could be regarded 'as a gi-gantic world-wide estate in bankruptcy of forty million square miles'. There would be plenty of pickings for the Rus-sians. This knowledge must have diminished the Prime Min-ister's pleasure at being showered with praise from Moscow.

The only people who seemed wholly pleased with 'Barba-rossa' were the American isolationists. They could now call members of 'Fight for Freedom' 'Communists' as well as 'crypto-British Imperialists', 'Merchants of Death', 'tools of In-ternational Jewry' and other epithets. They also felt more than ever that the Nazis were 'the wave of the future' now that they were (supposedly) demolishing Russia.

VII
The Organised Militant
Citizen

1

When total air warfare comes, a 'last stand' needs more than
brave armed forces and brilliant men of science. I have already
quoted J. B. Priestley about the network of voluntary associations which absorbed almost every able-bodied man and
woman not in uniform. The volunteers were a new type, which
Priestley called 'the organised militant citizen'.

The type flourished during the lonely year and under the
blitz. Few seemed to mind the nightly threat of death or dismemberment. They went about their work as if this were as
natural as delivering milk. Later, when the heat was off, people
became more like themselves and less praiseworthy. The
whoosh of bombs can be exhilarating. There is no exhilaration
about boredom and shabby clothes and monotonous food.
After December, 1941, nobody except the armed forces and
the merchant marine felt the imminence of death or captivity.
On the home front everyone felt the war was dragging on too
long, too drearily long. Even after D-Day in June of 1944, although we all knew we were winning, nothing except mounting casualties seemed to happen. This was a tribute to the
Wehrmacht in defeat, but no one felt pleased to pay.

While the citizens under the rain of bombs were enduring,

and creating, their finest hour, the Foreign Office was in limbo—'a place of neglect or oblivion'. How can you conduct Foreign Affairs with a country which does not believe you exist? Few governments, except Washington under Roosevelt, thought Britain durable until the blitz proved vain.

The official history, *British Foreign Policy in the Second World War*, puts the point tersely. Britain was struggling for existence: 'This limited the scope of British diplomatic action in two ways. Some countries thought a British collapse so certain that they would not listen to any suggestions from the Government; others were less sure of a German victory but through fear of German retaliation against themselves dared not give Britain support.'

With the Foreign Office in limbo and the army unarmed and the navy overstretched by war in all the oceans, Britain was lucky that so many rushed to organise themselves for total resistance.

'This is a War of the Unknown Warriors,' Churchill told Britain in the summer of 1940 . . . 'The whole of the warring nations are engaged, not only soldiers but the entire population, men, women and children. The fronts are everywhere. The trenches are dug in the towns and streets. Every village is fortified. Every road is barred. The front lines run through the factories. The workmen are soldiers with different weapons but the same courage.'

On May 22, 1940, Parliament had handed the Minister of Labour unusual powers. 'It is necessary that the Government should be given complete control over persons and property, not just some persons and some particular class of the community, but all persons, rich and poor, employer and workman, man or woman, and all property.' The Minister could direct any person to do any job for whatever hours and wages he saw fit. Ernest Bevin was Minister of Labour. He was the least likely man I have known to refrain from power or to permit malingering. The fact that he used his tyrant-rights sparingly is a proof that the British civilians had put themselves to work before the Government got round to telling them what to do.

All citizens were conscripted—women for the first time. The age limits stretched and stretched, both ways. In the end, everybody, male or female, from eighteen to sixty, was obliged to undertake some form of national service. (In the armed forces, the ages were eighteen to fifty-one.) Nevertheless, in five years Bevin only 'directed' a quarter of a million men and 88,000 women. For a nation of fifty million people, where everyone over adolescence was at work, these are tiny figures. And the 'directions' were mostly to move from an uncomfortable urban job to a more uncomfortable job in some isolated new factory. For the most part the over-forty civilians directed themselves and Bevin left them alone.

Such dedication was a result of life-or-death aerial warfare. Those who remember the First World War will know that even in England there was much 'business as usual'. In the United States that war scarcely bruised the civilian economy. People who took their coffee without sugar felt themselves part of the Great Event. In Hitler's war even Americans were deprived. The whole free world was waiting for American goods: synthetic rubber, petrol, airplanes, guns, landing-craft, merchant ships, etc., etc. The United States could not produce all that with one hand. Civilian consumption was diminished —but less than in any other nation at war. Anyone who half-laughed at the waste of food, matches, cigarettes and other priceless commodities at the American Red Cross hostels in England during 1943 and 1944 will remember the difference between being incommoded and being on the brink of hardship.

The days of improvisation and inspired amateurism on the home front stretched from the fall of France to the invasion of Russia. The people led themselves, with the help of Churchill's speeches. Traditional local government was not up to the sudden strain; full employment relieved the worker from most economic restraints. Throughout civilian life, the discipline of that year was mostly self-imposed, which is why people relished it. As Angus Calder reminds us, the air raid warden and the shop steward between them kept courage up by night and production by day. Had these two unofficial groups not been totally in the war, there might have come a lag—and if a lag had begun the blitz might have fulfilled Goering's hopes.

Or maybe the whole idea of a blitz is worthless. Berlin and other German towns seemed to prove this, when the Allies got round to flattening them.

Christabel Bielenberg was a niece of Lord Northcliffe, who married a German lawyer in 1934 and lived in Germany until after Hitler's war. Her husband and his closest friends were among the few true conspirators against Hitler. Most of them were destroyed. None of them were much impressed by the Allied counter-blitz of 1943–44 which seemed to us so important at the time. Christabel Bielenberg writes: 'I learned when I was in Berlin that those wanton, quite impersonal killings, that barrage from the air which mutilated, suffocated, burned and destroyed, didn't so much breed fear and a desire to bow before the storm, but rather a certain fatalistic cussedness, a dogged determination to survive and, if possible, help others to survive, whatever their politics, whatever their creed.'

The same complaint recurs throughout her fascinating book. The Bielenbergs and their friends were traitors to the Third Reich. The men believed it their duty, as Germans, to kill Hitler and the leading Nazis. They felt Germany would be disgraced if this necessary work were left to the Allies. They were unanimous in thinking the indiscriminate terror-raids a mistake: the more terror-raids the less hope for their own cause, since the raids united the people behind the régime.

This, like the clamour against 'unconditional surrender', might be an excuse for the failure of 'good Germans' to do anything useful. Yet the clear-eyed Anglo-Irish niece of Northcliffe was unlikely to be fooled by excuses. Her testimony is that the night-bombing of big cities, for the purpose of killing and frightening, prolonged the war. The more one contemplates the blitz over England, the more likely her story seems.

Imagine how a traitor-group in England (pledged to kill Churchill and his Cabinet) would have cursed Goering. His blitz not only united the people behind the Government, it united the people with themselves. So long as the high explosives and the incendiaries fell on rich and poor alike, and on famous towns and village schools[1] senselessly, maliciously, Disraeli's Two Nations were almost welded into One. The class system was suspended, its power never to be recovered as of old. (This was not a war-aim by the Government but a war-gift by Goering.) So my imagined traitors, while the blitz was on, could only complain about the stupidity of their friends the Germans, fold up their plans and wait. The Bielenbergs may have been right.

2

As Admiral Stark said regretfully, 'dollars cannot buy yesterday'; neither can legislation. When a crisis is at last admitted by a democracy, the necessary laws are passed and the necessary new powers are assumed; but for a long time nothing happens. Sometimes a ponderous new department has to be created and a lot of ponderous civil servants trained to man it. Or, as in the case of aircraft production and Lord Beaverbrook, a number of established departments have to be raided and driven half-daft so that the emergency may be met. The British people are good at what might be called official improvisation and the results are sometimes startling; but the word 'official' implies delay. If the problem is something less awe-inspiring than the production of Spitfires, the untrained en-

[1] The village of Petworth in West Sussex became almost as childless as Hamelin after the Pied Piper had taken his revenge. A scared German pilot, to gain speed, dumped his bombs during lesson-time on to the local school.

thusiasts can often fill the gap. The preservation of St Paul's
Cathedral is an example.

During the 1914–18 war St Paul's had been used as a shelter
from air raids. At the time of Munich, when war seemed certain, the cathedral staff thought that modern bombs, even
near-by, might bring the whole thing down, killing all inmates.
'We were most anxious', writes the Dean, 'to find out what the
authorities wanted us to do about closing the cathedral during
air raids.' The authorities had no idea what they wanted, although the Dean and one of his staff 'interviewed all the departments we could think of'. At last they found a harassed
little man who was in charge of the city's air raid protection.
'I don't think it matters much what you do,' was the helpful
answer; 'If there is a raid tonight we expect 30,000 casualties.'
The Dean comments, 'After that we ceased to worry.' They
got on with the business of caring for the cathedral in their
own way.

The first job was to find a commander, someone to put in
total charge. You cannot save a cathedral with a committee.
The surveyor, who had an unrivalled knowledge of the vast
building, was Godfrey Allen, F.R.I.B.A. He accepted the post,
which is doubtless why St Paul's exists today.

Extra water tanks were installed at all levels in case the
main water should fail (as it usually did). Many new doors
and stairs were built to speed fire-fighting, also one master-
shelter which was supposed to stand even if the whole building tumbled. And the famous 'Watch' of almost two hundred
volunteers was recruited and trained and led by Mr Allen.
These are small samples of what was done; but the commander
and his fellow-workers did save St Paul's, the most conspicu-
ous landmark in the City of London and the centre of the Luftwaffe's most furious raids.

The whole area round about was blasted and much of it
burned to the ground. Early on, the dome of the cathedral
received a direct hit and innumerable fires were started by
incendiaries. And as late as the night of April 16–17, 1941, the

Luftwaffe made a final attack on the cathedral. A high-explosive bomb hit the north transept. A land-mine drifted within a few feet of the east walls but did not explode. Somehow the 'band of brothers' who guarded the place mastered all this. They were guarding, not just another church, but something central to the concept of London for Christians and non-Christians alike. 'The Parish Church of the Commonwealth', it was often called.

The same spirit of never-give-in-to-the-war could take hilarious forms. A Richmond golf club in the summer of 1940, adopted these 'emergency rules':

'Players are asked to collect bomb and shell splinters to save these causing damage to the mowers.

'A ball moved by enemy action may be replaced as near as possible to where it lay or if lost or destroyed a ball may be dropped not nearer the hole without penalty.

'A player whose stroke is affected by the simultaneous explosion of a bomb or shell or by machine-gun fire may play another ball from the same place. Penalty one stroke.'

Presumably, if the player was wounded by machine-gun fire the committee might have remitted that penalty.

More seriously, Norman Longmate (who discovered those charming rules) records that in many clubs, where the fairways were obstructed with anti-landing barricades, 'an extra stroke was allowed if a ball hit one'. A golf club whose fairways were relatively flat was sure to have such obstructions, just as a farmer would have his best fields studded with great poles round which he would have to learn to plough.[2]

---

[2] In 1943 I was sent to America from London during the hottest weeks of a hot summer to travel the cornhog belt of the Middle West, to explain to incensed farmers why all the new, most mobile tractors (which they craved) were sent to England under Lend-Lease—an odd job for an author who was pretending to be a naval officer who was pretending to be a diplomat. I had been tutored on British farming for three weeks. My audiences were experts and asked angry-expert questions. I had only to say 'Sorry, they didn't give me the answer to that one' and all was forgiven. The mighty Mid-West saw me as a harmless ignoramus and went on supporting Lend-Lease.

3

The most famous of the volunteers doing all the jobs which nobody else seemed ready to do was the W.V.S. In June, 1938, in plenty of time to be ready when the bad days came, Lady Reading founded 'Women's Voluntary Services for Civil Defence,' calling upon 'every kind of woman in every sphere of life' to prepare to defend the homes and succour the civilians of Britain against the outrages of war. While newspaper proprietors and Privy Councillors were still dreaming of peace, the women of Britain were rallying round Stella Reading, learning and training to alleviate the impending pain. Sooner or later, almost every woman who was not in the armed forces or the factories worked at least part time for the W.V.S., 'the Women in Green'. By 1941 there were a million members, 200 of whom were paid.

Immobile women, who were in charge of too many children or too many infirm relatives, were found work within reach of home. Mobile women, if over-age for conscription, were learning new life-saving jobs.

Here was a triumph of organisation by Lady Reading and her staff. No other nation, including the Germans and the Russians in their worst hour, had so many women (in proportion to population) working in factories, fields and armed forces. These were the young and mobile, whom the Government conscripted. No other nation even tried to mobilise the not-young and the not-mobile on a large scale. Some women worked in their homes or in local part-time assembly plants. Thousands worked wherever the bombs were falling, feeding the rescue teams, guarding the rescued and building outdoor kitchens from the rubble of a destroyed street to feed the people who no longer had a house.

'Please do not hesitate', said Lady Reading to her County

Organisers in May, 1940, 'to take such lead as is demanded of
you . . . W.V.S. is looked upon as a strong, efficient machine
which can carry an immense load.'

The unexpected loads were the tests for the W.V.S.: 25,000
refugees from the Channel Islands; 12,000 civilians ordered
out of Gibraltar overnight; the irritating problems of women
and children streaming out of London and other centres under
the exact planning of the Minister of Transport and then
streaming back before the New Year because Hitler had not
yet found time to set fire to the great towns of England. A little
later came the problem of the orphaned children, evacuated
for the second time and suddenly without parents because
the Luftwaffe had scored a hit at home.

No Government, fighting for the nation's life, could have
dealt wisely with such problems; but the women of Britain
did, inspired by Stella Reading.

The message from the Chairman of the W.V.S. on its seventh
birthday, a month after the defeat of Germany, was an un-
derstatement: 'We have learned that it is no good talking
about things, we must do them . . . We have done work we
had never thought to approach and we have carried burdens
heavier than we knew existed.'

When Henry Morgenthau, Secretary of the Treasury, visited
London as Roosevelt's personal representative, he wrote in
his diaries (as condensed by John Morton Blum): 'What the
women in England were doing was just unbelievable. This was
true alike for women in the armed services and in the civilian
occupations, true of their housekeeping, their cooking and
work in the barracks, their managing of buses and motorcycles.
In the services, as one person put it, . . . they treat them like
men and they want to be treated like men. There is no nonsense about it . . . If it were not for the women England would
cave in today . . . The war for the women in England was a
hard, tough job; and do those people hate Hitler!'

Commander Firebrace, Chief of Fire Staff during the years
when every effort was made to burn London to the ground,

agrees with Morgenthau about the women enlisted in his dangerous service. 'Not every fireman', he writes, 'was enthusiastic about being detailed to train women auxiliaries, but the majority soon settled down to it. Most women liked being treated precisely as were the men—no distinctions made. They liked smartness and that touch of "click heels" which if not overdone, means a great deal in a disciplined service.'

By 1943 there were 27,300 women in the Fire Service. Commander Firebrace comments: 'There were in 1939 a few men who openly doubted whether women would stand up to bombing, to seeing their fire station being gradually ringed by fire and sticking to it, to being blown from their telephones by blast and still keeping communications open, to driving for long hours under dangerous and difficult conditions and not asking for a relief. This type of man is now extinct.'

John Strachey has an interesting gloss on women in the Hitler war. He had watched them at work as Air Raid Wardens, ambulance drivers, stretcher bearers, drivers of the W.V.S. mobile canteens which always turned up where the bombing was heaviest, etc. 'How appropriate it was that women—both in Civil Defence and in the Women's Auxiliary Corps attached to the Services—should be taking an unprecedently large part in a war against the Nazi power. For, after all, perhaps the most characteristic part of the Nazi faith was its insistence on the degradation of women. Whoever else might fail to realise what they were fighting for, no women should have any doubt. The outcome of the war would decide whether women were to hold and extend their grasp on full citizenship in the modern world, or were to go back to the admitted dependence of former centuries. It seemed . . . to be right and proper that they should take an ever increasing part in such a war.'

The official, Government-sponsored Civil Defence was slower than W.V.S. to get started; but it was longer in preparation and once it did get started it developed smoothly.

As early as 1924 the Committee of Imperial Defence asked

a young civil servant named John Anderson to head a sub-
committee to study Air Raid Precautions. In 1937 local authorities were told to submit their own plans for their own
districts. And in March, 1938, three months before Lady Reading made her appeal, the Home Secretary asked for a million
recruits for dangerous work in case of air raids. He didn't get
them. Air Raid Precautions were not taken seriously until after
Munich. In 1939 recruiting became brisk and training serious.
There was still ample time before the blitz; but Heaven help
the A.R.P. services if war had come in the month of Munich.

4

When the Luftwaffe, frustrated by Fighter Command, finally
turned on London, it met a Civil Defence which after a bit of
blood-letting became as efficient as possible. I am talking about
the men and women above ground, working among the
wounded and the corpses: the 'organised militant citizen'.
Whether the Government should, or could, have provided
masses of deep shelters, I do not know because I do not know
the priorities after the astounding German victories between
May 10 and May 30, 1940. Anyone who thinks that shattering
three weeks could have been foreseen must see himself as
wiser than any man alive at the time. Hitler was as surprised
as the London County Council. He should have been building
landing-craft. They should have been digging deep shelters.
In the end, Hitler's was the deadlier mistake.

When the raids began on London they lasted all night,
every night. There was a period of two months with only two
nights off. The wardens and the firemen and the stretcher
bearers and the mobile canteens from the W.V.S. and the experts who dug tunnels through the rubble wherever a voice
or a groan could be heard—all these were soon working together as a well-trained team. The wardens were responsible

for the co-ordination. A full-time paid warden had to be on
duty every night except one during the week, and on call all
day in case of an 'incident' by daylight. That charming,
neutral word 'incident' could mean anything from a rain of
incendiaries to a land-mine, to an hour-long pelting by a hundred bombers (but such peltings came only at night).

The full-time wardens were paid £3 5s a week if male, £2
if female—an absurd discrimination since women on the whole
were better than men, being calmer and more businesslike
when faced with blood and dismemberment.

Many wardens chose to be unpaid, in which case they were
on duty four nights out of five, but not on call during the day.
Anyone who tried to combine the unpaid job with day-time
work would soon be an over-weary man or woman; but
thousands did it. After all, the 'incidents' were widespread
and with good luck a warden might get several hours of sleep
toward dawn, several nights a week.

These wardens came from every branch of life and from
every sort of occupation, proving the talents and the zest for
leadership which are normally lost to the nation through
poverty or the wrong accent. This is what Priestley meant
by Britain being bombed and burned into democracy. When
the bombing and burning were diverted to Russia the democracy diminished.

John Strachey suggests it was the uniform that liberated the
hidden talents of so many 'militant citizens'. 'The instant an
individual is given even the simplest objective function,' he
writes, 'and becomes a member of an organised (and uni-
formed, this is notoriously important) group, the whole
burden of deciding whether or not on any particular occasion
to seek his or her own safety is automatically removed. While
one is functionless one is continually irritated by such questions as "Isn't it really very silly to stay upstairs (or to go out)
in this degree of blitz?" The instant the individual has become
a warden, ambulance driver, member of the auxiliary fire

service, rescue or demolition squad, or stretcher bearer, this question is, nine times out of ten, settled for him or her.'

This was true of the Home Guard, who felt happy when they got a uniform or an arm band, even if they had no weapon more lethal than a pickaxe or one of Churchill's beer bottles. And it was true of the W.V.S. whose green uniforms were a comfort to themselves and also to any victim of the multifarious troubles which an 'incident' can produce.

An important discovery by these 'militant citizens', as they felt their way toward greater efficiency, was that in a major 'incident' they must quickly appoint an 'incident officer': a warden who stays in one place, under a blue flag by day or a blue light by night, to co-ordinate the work of all the amateurs and professionals who swarm about. The geography of the area may have been changed by bombs so that even residents lose their way. In the darkness nobody knows who anybody is, or what they are doing, or why. No lights are allowed except the faint blue where the 'incident officer' stands. His job is impossible: this is one of the ways whereby natural leaders were discovered among the most unexpected people. Once discovered they were cherished so long as the war lasted.

5

Those who joined the Auxiliary Fire Service in London did not have to improvise. They had joined an élite corps and had only to try to emulate the professionals. Skilled drivers could be useful at once, because when the war began 2,381 taxis were hired by the London Fire Service to tow light trailer pumps. These pumps were delivered in large quantities in October, 1939, but without vehicles to pull them.

Also twenty new fire boats were ordered in 1938 and ten in 1939. The few recruits who knew the tricky waters of the Thames had a job at once; but for the most part, since the London Fire Service was as well trained as the Guards, the new boys and girls struggled like a freshly commissioned officer in the Wavy Navy to look and sound like an old hand overnight.

Oddly, the new boys and girls—Navy, Army, Air and Fire—did contrive in many cases to become old hands overnight. This did not always please the professionals, the genuine old hands who insisted it took at least twenty years to know what they knew.

The Civil Defence Services as a whole, all the diverse groups I have mentioned, if taken as a single Civil Defence Corps, are something new in military history, something called into being by indiscriminate bombing of civilians. The Corps was partly men and partly women doing the same jobs, partly paid workers and partly volunteers doing the same jobs. Organised and controlled by local authorities, the members of this strange Corps were never subject to the Army Act or to any discipline except their own. No threat hung over a slack Civil Defence worker except the threat of not being wanted any more. When one remembers the disciplinary powers of the armed forces, this is an impressive thought.

Epilogue

1

When Germany invaded Russia, Britain had 2,250,000 men in the army, 395,000 in the navy, 662,000 in the air force and a fair scattering of women in all three services. The Russians soon had an army of about 8,000,000—rising to 12,500,000 (in spite of fearful losses) by the end of the war. So why do I say in my Preface that Britain rather than Russia stood between Hitler and the dominion of the West?

First, Fighter Command and the Navy stopped Hitler from invading England, so he had to attack Russia with an army to his rear, with a navy blockading Europe and with bomber raids on his big towns—raids which were at last becoming troublesome.

Second, in North Africa and Greece and the Mediterranean, the British destroyed Germany's ally, caused Hitler to divert his forces and delayed his invasion of Russia by an all-important month or six weeks.

Third, remember the unsung people in my last chapter: the Civil Defence Corps and the millions they were trying to defend—'the Many', who in their way were as important as 'the Few'. No bomber-war can ever be won if 'the Many' refuse. The Luftwaffe, though misdirected, was a mighty weapon. The mere sight of it in peace-time paralysed the will and the judgment of a brave man: Lindbergh. The whole of this machine was thrown for nine months against the civilian townspeople of Great Britain: the first trial of the Douhet theory of warfare. By the end of the nine months the townspeople were disciplined and organised and unafraid.

2

As I said in my Preface, the British could not have won the war alone. There can be no doubt about that. A lot of people were needed to overcome the fury of the Nazis; but there would not have been any war to win or lose had Britain joined France in surrender in the summer of 1940. Imagine a Britain invaded, half-depopulated, with all her resources in the hands of the Germans; Hitler free to deal with Russia at his leisure and the United States unable to land in Europe, or bomb Europe, or hinder the Nazis in any way, without a base in Britain. Furthermore, without the example of Britain to astonish them, Americans might have gone on sleeping until the Western and the Eastern tyrants were ready for the final carve-up. And the tyrants would have had total control of the seas.

Or the United States might have appropriated many billions and tried to prepare for defence; but dollars 'cannot buy yesterday'. Great Britain could; or at least she could buy a lot of time for her laggard friends—seventeen months from the collapse of France to Pearl Harbor.

I think Churchill himself, for all his valour and his uncompromising words, knew that Britain could not win alone. The news of Pearl Harbor came to England on a Sunday evening. Churchill was dining in the country with two Americans: John Winant the Ambassador, and Averell Harriman the President's Special Representative for Lend-Lease. They telephoned to Roosevelt and then (according to his book) the Prime Minister mused as follows: 'So we had won after all. After seventeen months of lonely fighting, . . . we had won the war. England would live; Britain would live . . . We should not be wiped out. Our history would not come to an end. We might not even have to die as individuals . . . Many disasters, immeasurable cost and tribulation lay ahead, but there was no more doubt about the end.'

There was doubt, in fact. Within sixteen months the U-boats were almost to starve Britain. And how could the United States try to reconquer Europe, without England? We should be glad that Churchill was not bothered, in his hour of relief, by premonitions.

3

Maybe the tyrant state will prove to be 'the wave of the future'. Man may find himself too harassed by his own inventions to take the trouble to remain free. This catastrophe, if it is fated, has now been postponed for several generations. We have been given another chance, and we have been given it by the people of Great Britain. I would find it churlish if we were to forget this, and not even say thank you.

Bibliography

Anon, *The Pomp of Power*, Tenth Edition, London undated (1922?)

Astley, Joan Bright, *The Inner Circle*, London, 1971

Avon, the Rt Hon. Earl of, *The Eden Memoirs: Facing the Dictators*, London, 1962

——, *The Eden Memoirs: The Reckoning*, London, 1965

Balfour, Sir John, *Unpublished Memoirs*

Barnett, Corelli, *The Sword-Bearers*, London, 1963

Baudouin, Paul, *Neuf mois au Governement*, Paris, 1948 (English translation: The Private Diaries of Paul Baudouin, London, 1948)

Beaufre, André, *Le Drame de 1940*, Paris, 1965

Benoist-Méchin, J., *Sixty Days that Shook the West*, London, 1956

Berl, Emmanuel, *La Fin de la IIIe Republique*, Paris, 1968

Berlin, Isaiah, *Mr Churchill in 1940*, London, 1964

Bielenberg, Christabel, *The Past is Myself*, London, 1968

Blum, John Morton, *Roosevelt and Morgenthau* (Revision and Condensation, from the Morgenthau Diaries), Boston, 1970

Bonnefous, Édouard, *La Course vers l'Abime: 1938–1940*, Paris, 1967

Bouthillier, Y., *Le Drame de Vichy*, 2 vols, Paris, 1950

Brogan, D. W., *The Development of Modern France*, London, 1940

Bryant, Arthur, *The Turn of the Tide, 1939–1942* (based on the Diaries and Notes of Field-Marshal the Viscount Alanbrooke), London, 1957

Bullock, Alan, *The Life and Times of Ernest Bevin*, vol. 2: *Minister of Labour 1940–1945*, London, 1967

——, *Hitler, a Study in Tyranny* (revised edition), London, 1962

——, *Hitler and the Origins of the Second World War*, published by British Academy, 1967

Burns, James MacGregor, *Roosevelt: The Soldier of Freedom 1940–1945*, London, 1970

Butler, R. A. (now Lord Butler), *The Art of the Possible*, London, 1971

Cadogan, Sir Alexander, *Diaries*, London, 1971

Calder, Angus, *The People's War*, London, 1969

Calder, Ritchie (now Lord Ritchie-Calder), *Carry on London*, London, 1941

——, *Lessons of London*, London, 1941

Carr, E. H., *The Twenty Years' Crisis*, London, 1958

Chadwin, Mark Lincoln, *The Hawks of World War Two*, University of North Carolina, 1968

Chapman, Guy, *Why France Collapsed*, London, 1968

Churchill, Winston, *War Speeches*, vol. I; *Into Battle*, London, 1941

——, *The Second World War*, vols 2 and 3, London, 1949, 1950

Ciano's Diary, 1939–1943, edited by Malcolm Muggeridge, London, 1947

Clemenceau, G., *Grandeur and Misery of Victory*, London, 1930

Cooper, Alfred Duff, *Old Men Forget*, London, 1953

——, *The Second World War, First Phase*, London, 1939

Croom-Johnson, Norman, *Diary, 1905–1961*

Darwin, Bernard, *War on the Line*, London, 1946

De Gaulle, Charles, *Vers L'Armée de Métier*, Paris, 1934

——, *War Mémoires*, vol. 1, London, 1955

Douglas-Hamilton, James, *Motive for a Mission*, London, 1971

Douhet, General Giulio, *The Command of the Air*, London, 1943 (Italian edition in early 1920s)

Farrer, David, *The Sky's the Limit*, London, 1943

——, *G-for God Almighty*, London, 1969

Feis, Herbert, *Churchill, Roosevelt, Stalin*, Princeton, 1957

——, *The Road to Pearl Harbor*, Princeton, 1950

Fischer, Fritz, *Grift nach der Weltmacht*, Dusseldorf, 1961

Fitzgibbon, Constantine, *The Blitz*, London, 1957

Fleming, Peter, *Invasion 1940*, London, 1957

Fuller, Major-General J. F. C., *The Second World War*, London, 1948

Galbraith, John Kenneth, *Albert Speer was the Man to See*, New York Times Book Review, Jan. 10, 1971

Galland, Adolf, *The First and the Last*, London, 1955

(Gallup Polls) *Public Opinion 1935–46*, Princeton, 1951

Gamelin, Maurice, *Servir, Les Armées Françaises de 1940*, 3 vols, Paris, 1946

Gellhorn, Martha, *The Face of War*, London, 1959

Gibbs, Air-Marshal Sir Gerald, *Survivor's Story*, London, 1956

Gilbert, M., *The Roots of Appeasement*, London, 1964

Edited by Willi Boelcke (translated by Ewald Osers), *The Secret Conferences of Dr Goebbels, October 1939–1943*, London, 1970

Goodhart, Philip, *Fifty Ships that Saved the World*, London, 1965

Graves, Charles, *The Home Guard of Britain*, London, 1943

——, *Women in Green*, London, 1948

Griffiths, Richard, *Marshal Pétain*, London, 1970

Grunberger, Richard, *A Social History of the Third Reich*, London, 1971

Guderian, Heinz, *Panzer Leader*, London, 1952

The Diplomatic Diaries of Oliver Harvey, 1937–1940, edited by John Harvey, London, 1970

Hitler, Adolf, *Hitler's Secret Book*, London, 1963

——, *Hitler's Table Talk* (introduced by H. R. Trevor-Roper), London, 1953

——, *Hitler's War Directives* (introduction by H. R. Trevor-Roper), London, 1964

Hofer, W. J., *War Premeditated*, London, 1954

Horne, Alistair, *To Lose a Battle, France, 1940*, London, 1969

Howarth, David, *Trafalgar, The Nelson Touch*, London, 1969

Hull, Cordell, *Memoirs*, 2 vols, New York, 1948

Ismay, General, the Lord, *Memoirs*, London, 1960

Jacobsen, H. A., *Nationalsozialistische Aussenpolitik, 1933–1939*, Frankfurt, 1969

Johnson, B. S., *The Evacuees*, London, 1968

Johnson, Walter, *1600 Pennsylvania Avenue*, Boston, 1960

Jones, Tom, *A Diary with Letters*, Oxford, 1954

Keynes, J. M., *The Economic Consequences of the Peace*, London, 1919

——, *Essays in Persuasion*, London, 1952

——, *Essays in Biography*, London, 1951

Kimball, Warren F., *The Most Unsordid Act*, Baltimore, 1968

Kirkpatrick, I., *Mussolini, A Study of Power*, New York, 1964

Lampe, David, *The Last Ditch*, London, 1968

Langer, L. and Gleason, S. E., *The Challenge of Isolation*, New York, 1952

Le Chêne, Evelyn, *Mathausen*, London, 1971

Liddell Hart, B. H., *The Tanks*, London, 1959

——, *History of the Second World War*, London, 1970

Lindbergh, Charles H., *The Wartime Journals*, New York, 1970

Lockhart, Bruce, *Comes the Reckoning*, London, 1947

Longmate, Norman, *How We Lived Then*, London, 1971

MacInnes, C. M., *Bristol at War*, London, 1962

Mackenzie, Sir Compton, *Greece in My Life*, London, 1960

MacLeod, I., *Neville Chamberlain*, London, 1961

Maillaud, Pierre, *France*, Oxford, 1942

Mann, Thomas, *Letters*, 2 vols (translated by Richard and Clara Winston), London, 1970

Martin, Kingsley, *Autobiography*, 2 vols, London, 1966, 1968

Marwick, Arthur, *Britain in the Century of Total War*, London, 1968

Matthews, W. R., *Saint Paul's Cathedral in Wartime*, London, 1946

Maurois, André, *Tragedy in France*, New York, 1940

———, *A History of France* (translated H. L. Binsse), London, 1949

Michel, Henri, *La Guerre de l'Ombre*, Paris, 1971

Middleton, Drew, *The Sky Suspended*, London, 1960

Montgomery of Alamein, *Memoirs*, London and New York, 1958

Morison, Samuel Eliot, *The Two-Ocean War*, Boston, 1963

Mosley, Leonard, *Backs to the Wall*, London, 1971

Mowrer, Edgar Ansel, *Triumph and Turmoil*, New York, 1968

Namier, L. B., *In the Nazi Era*, London, 1952

Nicolson, Harold, *Diaries and Letters 1939–1945*, London, 1967

O'Brien, T. H., *Civil Defence*, London, 1955

Offner, Arnold A., *American Appeasement*, Harvard University Press, 1969

Orwell, George, *The Lion and the Unicorn*, London, 1941

Rawnsley, C. F., with Robert Wright, *Night Fighter*, London, 1957

Report of Captain Miles Reid, Liaison Officer I (French) Army, June 6, 1940

Reynaud, Paul, *La France a Sauvé l'Europe*, Paris, 1947

Richards, Denis, *The Royal Air Force, 1939–1945,* vol. 1: *The Fight at Odds,* London, 1953

Richmond, Admiral Sir Hubert W., *The Invasion of Britain, An Account of Plans, Attempts and Counter-Measures from 1546 to 1918,* London, 1941

Rommel, E., *The Rommel Papers,* edited by B. H. Liddell Hart, London, 1953

Ryan, Cornelius, *The Last Battle,* London, 1966

Sampson, Anthony, *Anatomy of Britain Today,* London, 1965

Schwarzschild, L., *World in Trance,* London, 1943

Shirer, William L., *The Rise and Fall of the Third Reich,* New York, 1960

Spears, Edward, *Assignment to Catastrophe,* 2 vols, London, 1954

Speer, Albert, *Inside the Third Reich,* London, 1970

Strachey, John, *Post D,* London, 1941

Taylor, A. J. P., *English History 1914–45,* London, 1965

——, *The Origins of the Second World War* (new introduction), London, 1963

Taylor, Telford, *The Breaking Wave,* London, 1967

Templewood, Viscount, *Ambassador on Special Mission,* London, 1946

Thompson, Lawrence, *1940: Year of Legend, Year of History,* London, 1966

Titmuss, R. M., *Problems of Social Policy,* London, 1950–51

Townsend, Peter, *Duel of Eagles,* London, 1970

Wallace, Euan, *Diary 1939–1940*

Werner, Herbert A., *Iron Coffins,* London, 1970

Weygand, M., *Recalled to Service,* London, 1952

Wheatley, R. A. A., *Operation Sea-Lion,* London, 1958

Wheeler-Bennett, John, *The Nemesis of Power,* London, 1953

——, *King George VI,* London, 1956

Williams, John, *The Ides of May,* London, 1968

Woodward, Sir Llewellyn, *British Foreign Policy in the Second World War,* vol. 1, London, 1970

Woolf, Leonard, *Autobiography of the Years 1939–1969*, London, 1969

Wormser, Georges, *Georges Mandel*, Paris, 1967

Wright, Robert, *Dowding and the Battle of Britain*, London, 1969

——, *Night Fighter* (with C. F. Rawnsley), London, 1957

Wykeham, Peter, *Fighter Command*, London, 1960

Index

From June 22, 1940, when France surrendered to the Germans, until June 22, 1941, when Hitler invaded Russia, Britain alone stood against the German conquest of Europe. Herbert Agar's theme is that this period of hardly credible survival saved the Western world; the inspiration of this book is his strong conviction that the full significance of that year is not completely appreciated even now.

Mr. Agar focuses in depth on the historic months and the crucial events of that year, setting them in context and describing them vividly (*the most important non-event of 1940 was the invasion of England*). He quotes little-known reactions against some of the prominent people who believed that Britain was doomed. And he also quotes many of the legendary figures of the era as they spoke of legendary events; General "Hap" Arnold of the